"This excellent book offers a practical, concise understanding of how emotionally immature (EI) parents impact your feelings, thoughts, and behavior. With specific examples and exercises, you can learn how to express yourself and reduce fear and self-doubt to reclaim your right to your own emotional health and well-being. The depth of Gibson's therapeutic skills, sound psychological principles, and practical tools make this a must-read for anyone whose life has been challenged by the emotional immaturity of others. A valuable resource for the general public as well as professionals!"

—**Louise B. Lubin, PhD**, licensed clinical psychologist, and retired
    community faculty at Eastern Virginia Medical School

"Most everyone emerges from their childhood with a few emotional scars, anxieties, or insecurities. However, many children sustain serious emotional wounds when they have been raised by insensitive, self-absorbed, and controlling parents. Young children or adolescents in these situations can't see the big picture, are powerless to fight back, and often blame themselves for their predicament—locking in their emotional wounds for a lifetime.

Fortunately, the brilliance of Gibson's book sheds the light of understanding and provides the keys to healing for countless recovering individuals. This book is readable, relevant, grounded in solid science, and yet so accessible to the person searching for answers and healing from their wounds. It is a must-read for every student of human behavior and every mental health professional."

—**Dan W. Briddell, PhD**, licensed and board-certified clinical
    psychologist with over forty years of clinical practice experience,
    and author of *The Love Bug and Other Tales of Psychotherapy*

"In her newest book, Lindsay Gibson provides a beautifully written, easy-to-understand guidebook for all those who have had to struggle with being raised by EI parents. Gibson takes the reader through a straightforward, step-by-step approach, defining and explaining what EI parents look like, and how their conscious and unconscious behaviors have powerful and lasting effects on their children.

Using case studies, interactive written exercises, and a comprehensive Bill of Rights, Gibson empowers those who have been raised by EI parents to fully reclaim their authentic selves."

—**Kenneth A. Siegel, PhD**, clinical psycholog[...]
    of experience

"*Recovering from Emotionally Immature Parents* is a must-read for any adult who has ever struggled with a parental relationship, as well as therapists who expect to skillfully guide clients toward creating their own best lives. Reading Lindsay Gibson's masterful book is like spending time under the care of a gifted, grounded, and compassionate psychologist. It will broaden every reader's self-concept and strengthen his or her self-confidence. Beginning to end, it is filled with brilliant translations and applications of therapeutic concepts to the world of real, lived experiences."

—**Gretchen LeFever Watson, PhD**, clinical psychologist,
      professor at Ross University School of Medicine, and author of
      Your Patient Safety Survival Guide

"What a gift! After spending forty years talking with clients about the issues and solutions Lindsay Gibson addresses in this extraordinary book, finally there's one highly readable resource that provides a complete, in-depth look at what every client needs to know. Clear and concise explanations alongside extremely helpful exercises make this book an absolute must-read for the multitudes that experience the challenge of EI parents. Not just a book for the children of EI parents, but a fantastic one-stop resource for anyone dealing with a core set of problems we all actually struggle with in the majority of our adult relationships."

—**David Gordon, PhD**, clinical psychologist in private practice
      in Norfolk, VA; author of *Mindful Dreaming*; and founder of
      the Dreamwork Institute

"This book is a gift for those who have grown up with an EI parent. Gibson gets it—and she will help you feel seen and known in a way that you likely never felt with your parent. You'll be able to put words to your pain, so you can understand it, work through it, and ultimately separate from it as you work toward building relationships with yourself and others that will be more emotionally fulfilling. It is clear how much she genuinely cares for her clients and readers, and wants to support them in their journey."

—**Kathy Nguyen Li, PsyD**, licensed psychologist, and owner of
      Sage Counseling, PLLC, in Washington, D.C.

"For those who have lived their lives in the shadow of their EI parent's pain—Gibson teaches, with clarity and comfort, that who you are today is quite different from who and what you were taught to believe. She gives you permission to leave your parent's issues with them—to free yourself of ownership of their thoughts, feelings, and behaviors. Gibson has offered a gift! Embrace it and look to your new future with peace and the power of the true you!"

—**Pamela Brewer, MSW, PhD, LCSW-C**, psychotherapist; host of *MyNDTALK with Dr. Pamela Brewer*, a daily relationship and mental health podcast/broadcast

"A rare book that goes beyond self-help and provides true therapy. Gibson's presence is felt throughout, breaking through the reader's emotional isolation and providing gentle, concrete guidance through a daunting journey. An intelligent and generous work."

—**Laurie Helgoe, PhD**, author of *Introvert Power* and *Fragile Bully*

"*Recovering from Emotionally Immature Parents* is a true gift to readers who have difficulty acknowledging the legitimacy of their needs and feelings because their EI parents unconsciously placed their own needs front and center during the readers' formative years. Clearly formulated and chock-full of useful case illustrations and written exercises, this book vividly conveys the dynamics that leave children burdened by emotional imperatives that are not their own. By helping readers experience the compassion their parents couldn't convey, Gibson guides the reader to a treasure trove: the long-awaited experience of autonomy, authenticity, and vitality!"

—**Sarah Y. Krakauer, PsyD**, author of *Treating Dissociative Identity Disorder*

"Lindsay Gibson has again written a valuable book in *Recovering from Emotionally Immature Parents*. It contains extensive wisdom, thoughts, and tools for searching one's inner experiences, self-talk, and feelings from growing up with EI parents. This book is a resource for both individuals on a personal journey and therapists, in the human quest to heal life's wounds and grow into a more joyful and fulfilled life. Gibson's compassionate guidance is well researched with individual stories to enhance our understanding. She closes with a Bill of Rights for Adult Children of EI parents that is helpful for anyone in conflicted relationships."

> —**Mary Ann Kearley, CNS, LPC**, clinical nurse specialist
> in mental health, and licensed professional counselor in
> private practice in Chesapeake, VA

"Lindsay Gibson's latest book, *Recovering from Emotionally Immature Parents*, is a page-turner—a lively exploration along the path of losing and reclaiming oneself. With depth and research, Gibson grounds her many practical and creative suggestions with the fallout of family dynamics that cause us to lose our 'emotional autonomy.' If you've ever squirmed in an interpersonal situation, you will have tools for that too. Gibson shows that change is best served by self-connection over self-correction. Positivity and confidence can replace negativity and guilt. Gibson's own humility, striking clarity, and openness invite readers into a mindset of challenges and comfort. In writing this book, she acknowledges her dream of seeing readers gain the knowledge to truly be themselves."

> —**Lynn Zoll, EdD**, clinical psychologist with over thirty-five years
> of experience and a private practice in Virginia Beach, VA

"I loved Lindsay Gibson's innovative look at EI parenting from her perspective as a seasoned clinician who sees the continuing effects of earlier parenting play out in her patients' adult lives. Her clinical examples are deeply moving and encourage the use of the practical therapeutic exercise tools she provides in each chapter to break long-formed habits, and as a result, foster a true self-view. This book is highly needed at a time when we seem to have forgotten the values of self-reflection and honesty."

> —**Kathrin Hartmann, PhD**, psychotherapist, and professor at
> Eastern Virginia Medical School in Norfolk, VA

"In her latest book, Lindsay Gibson provides a unique glimpse into the inner workings of the EI mind and soul. She masterfully describes the challenges involved in relating to these people, and then guides the reader on a focused journey toward reclaiming their sense of Self.

Complex psychological concepts and skills are portrayed in a crystal-clear manner, leading the reader out of entrapment and into empowering relationships with themselves and others.

This book is a rare gem! I can't wait to share it with anyone interested in staying connected with the spark within themselves, and living in a transformational way!"

—**Kim Forbes, MEd, LCSW, ACSW**, owner of Still Point Psychotherapy; psychotherapist in private practice for twenty-five years in Virginia Beach, VA; and student and teacher of psychological and spiritual transformation

Recovering
from
Emotionally
Immature
Parents

Practical Tools to Establish
Boundaries & Reclaim
Your Emotional Autonomy

LINDSAY C. GIBSON, PsyD

New Harbinger Publications, Inc.

Publisher's Note

All the case examples in this book come from people who gave their permission to include their stories and quotes in this work. The identifying data of psychotherapy clients has been thoroughly disguised, and in some cases combined to preserve maximum confidentiality. Examples used were representative of many other client experiences as well, and were chosen for their universality.

While books such as this can be tremendously helpful, there is no substitute for psychotherapy, support groups, or other forms of face-to-face help. This book is not intended to be a substitute for psychotherapy, but an adjunct to it. Readers who feel the need are encouraged to seek out a psychotherapist who can help them work through the issues that may come up in reading this book.

NEW HARBINGER PUBLICATIONS is a registered trademark of New Harbinger Publications, Inc.

Distributed in Canada by Raincoast Books

Copyright © 2019 by Lindsay C. Gibson
New Harbinger Publications, Inc.
5674 Shattuck Avenue
Oakland, CA 94609
www.newharbinger.com

Cover design by Amy Shoup

Acquired by Tesilya Hanauer

Edited by Gretel Hakanson

FSC
www.fsc.org
MIX
Paper from
responsible sources
FSC® C011935

Library of Congress Cataloging-in-Publication Data

Names: Gibson, Lindsay C., author.
Title: Recovering from emotionally immature parents : practical tools to establish boundaries and reclaim your emotional autonomy / Lindsay C. Gibson, PsyD.
Description: Oakland, CA : New Harbinger Publications, Inc., [2019] | Includes bibliographical references.
Identifiers: LCCN 2019022147 (print) | LCCN 2019981266 (ebook) | ISBN 9781684032525 (paperback) | ISBN 9781684032532 (pdf) | ISBN 9781684032549 (epub)
Subjects: LCSH: Parent and adult child. | Adult children of dysfunctional families--Mental health. | Emotional maturity. | Dysfunctional families--Psychological aspects.
Classification: LCC HQ755.86 .G53 2019 (print) | LCC HQ755.86 (ebook) | DDC 306.874--dc23
LC record available at https://lccn.loc.gov/2019022147
LC ebook record available at https://lccn.loc.gov/2019981266

Printed in the United States of America

25   24   23

15   14   13   12   11   10   9

For Skip
To infinity and beyond

Contents

Introduction

One day listening to a client talk about her dad, I realized that her father wasn't just inappropriate and abusive; he was pathologically *immature*. Her father had the impetuosity and egocentrism of a very young child, with no thought for his impact on her. At an emotional level, he was like a giant toddler—at best, a fourteen-year-old. I thought of how many psychotherapy clients I'd had whose childhoods were overshadowed by this kind of parental unpredictability and emotional overreactivity. They grew up as captives of emotionally immature parents—psychological infants armed with rigid authority and a powerful adult body. That day I saw these parents differently, stripped of all their false authority and revealed for the bullies they were.

Other clients had emotionally immature (EI) parents who were better behaved but were so aloof—even outright rejecting—that their children grew up feeling emotionally lonely and connection-deprived. Although these parents often looked competent and dependable on the outside, they were so self-preoccupied and limited in empathy that they couldn't engage with their children. Still other clients' parents were pleasant enough but betrayed the child by absenting themselves whenever the child had a real problem or needed protection.

Whatever their differences in individual behaviors, my clients' emotionally immature parents were the same under the skin: all lacked in empathy, all were self-involved, and all could not sustain a satisfying emotional connection with their children. Overall, many of my clients grew up in a family atmosphere characterized by conflict, mockery, and a lack of emotional intimacy.

Paradoxically, many EI parents can behave like real adults in other ways, functioning well at work or in their social group. From the outside, it was hard to believe they could cause such misery at home for their children.

As children, my clients were deeply confused by their parents' contradictory personalities. The only thing that made sense was to blame themselves. Those who felt mistreated or overlooked as children figured it was their fault for not being lovable or interesting enough. These clients saw their emotional needs as illegitimate, felt guilty for being angry at their parents, and minimized or made excuses for their parents' behavior. ("Sure, they hit me, but so did a lot of parents in those days.")

The Problem with Emotionally Immature Parents

A childhood spent with EI parents can lead to long-lasting feelings of emotional loneliness, as well as ambivalence about relationships in general. Emotional loneliness is the result of feeling unseen and unresponded to, no matter how hard you try to communicate and connect. In adulthood, these children were often attracted to unsatisfying, disappointing partners and friends who seemed very familiar in their self-involvement and refusal to connect at a deeper emotional level.

When I teach clients about EI parents, many recognize their own histories. It's like a light bulb going on. It explains a parent whose love felt self-centered and who rejected their child's attempts at deeper emotional connection. Once they understand their parents' emotional immaturity, pivotal moments in childhood make sense to them at last. Seeing their parents' limitations more objectively, they no longer have to be prisoners of their parents' immaturity.

It's not just actual abuse that's harmful. The whole parenting approach of these parents is emotionally unhealthy, creating a climate of anxiety and untrustworthiness between parent and child. They treat children in such superficial, coercive, and judgmental ways that they undermine their children's ability to trust their own thoughts and feelings, thereby restricting the development of their children's intuition, self-guidance, efficacy, and autonomy.

As a child of an EI parent, you may have learned to shut yourself down in order not to upset your parent's emotional applecart. This is because your spontaneity might easily offend a thin-skinned EI parent. The intense reactivity of EI parents trains their children to be inhibited, passive, and acquiescent instead of nurturing their individuality and trust in others. In order to get along with these parents, it's easier in the short run to tune out who you really are and what you really want. But in the long run, you end up burdened by obligation, guilt, shame, and feeling trapped in your family role. The good news is that once you understand these parents and their effects, your life will be your own again.

The Purpose of This Book

Understanding how parental emotional immaturity has affected you is what this book is all about. Until you grasp your parent's psychological limitations, you may blame yourself wrongly or keep hoping for changes they won't make. This book will help you see what you've been up against while understanding your parent in the deepest possible way.

You are going to learn to name and explain EI characteristics and behaviors that have never been popularly defined. My aim in writing this book is to give you a language for everything that goes on in EI relationships, both what happens *between* you and them, and what happens *inside* yourself as you try to cope with them. Once you can name it, you can deal with it. The impact of emotionally immature persons (EIPs) doesn't have to rule your life. You can figure out their effect on you and neutralize it.

Throughout the book, you'll also find writing exercises to strengthen your self-awareness and gain insight into your experiences with EI parents and other EIPs. I hope you find these interactive exercises both enlightening and fun.

The Timeliness of Understanding Emotional Immaturity

This topic of emotional immaturity has never been more important. EI behavior is widespread these days, and EIPs cause enormous suffering in all walks of life. Because EIPs insist on dominating and being the center of importance, they don't leave room or resources for others to be fully themselves. Their me-first entitlement and self-justifications negate the rights of other people, giving them free rein for abuse, harassment, prejudice, exploitation, and corruption of all types.

Unfortunately, the lack of self-questioning in EI leaders can make them seem strong and confident, enticing followers to support agendas not in their best interests and almost solely for the benefit of the leader. Our vulnerability to self-centered authority starts in childhood when EI parents teach us that our thoughts are not as worthwhile as their thoughts and that we should accept whatever our parent tells us. It's easy to see how EI parenting could turn out children who later fall prey to extremism, exploitation, or even cults.

Learning about emotional immaturity will help you understand and deal with all manner of EI behavior, regardless of its source. The EIP in your life might be a parent, significant other, child, sibling, employer, customer, or anyone else. The interpersonal dynamics will be the same, whether inside the family or outside. All the methods that work with EI parents will work with other EIPs as well.

Overview of Topics

The first half of this book, part I, will focus on what you've been up against, describing what it's like to grow up with EI parents—or to be in a relationship with any EIP—and what you can do about it.

In chapter 1, we'll explore what it's like having a relationship with your EI parent. You'll learn about their hallmark *emotionally immature relationship system* (EIRS) and how they seek to make you responsible for their self-esteem and emotional stability. You'll also find out possible reasons why they turned out as they did.

Chapter 2 describes EI personality characteristics in detail. You'll also learn to spot EI *emotional coercions* and *emotional takeovers*, and how EIPs use self-doubt, fear, shame, and guilt in you in order to maintain their central role in the relationship.

In chapter 3, we'll explore what it's been like for you to try to have an emotionally satisfying relationship with your EI parent. We'll look at different types of EI parents and why they pull back from closeness. You'll learn how to see your EI parents more objectively, mourn what you didn't get, and move toward a more compassionate and loyal relationship with yourself, as well as others.

Chapter 4 shows you how to avoid emotional takeovers by EIPs by questioning their reality distortions and emotional emergencies. You'll learn how to set appropriate boundaries, as well as when and how to respond to their demands for help. You'll see how their interpersonal pressure can disconnect you from yourself, making you take responsibility for their happiness in spite of knowing better.

In chapter 5, you'll learn exactly what to say and do as the most effective responses to classic EI behaviors. You'll learn how to sidestep their pressure, lead the interaction, and stop them from taking over.

Chapter 6 shows the countless little ways that EI parents and other EIPs undermine your self-confidence and trust in your intuitions. EI parents and EIPs are hostile toward your inner life by mocking and invalidating your perceptions, thoughts, and feelings. In this chapter, you will learn how to be immune to this shaming by staying loyal to your inner experience.

In the second half, part II, of the book, we will shift from understanding and dealing with EIPs to strengthening your individuality in spite of them. As you focus more on your own growth, you'll be reversing the effects of growing up with EI parents.

In chapter 7, you'll see why valuing your inner world is crucial to reestablishing a solid relationship with yourself. With new loyalty to your inner self, you'll trust yourself and welcome your feelings as invaluable information about what needs your attention.

Chapter 8 shows you how to renounce EI-indoctrinated thinking to make room for your own mind. You'll learn to undo the self-doubt caused by critical EI parents who dismissed any viewpoints different from theirs. As you clear your mind of mental clutter from old EI influences, you'll have fewer obsessive worries and less self-criticism.

In chapter 9, you'll update and broaden your self-concept. It's unlikely that EI parents would've helped you develop an accurate, confident self-image. Instead, they're more likely to have taught you to be submissive, leading you to see other people's needs and feelings as more important than your own. As you update your self-concept, you'll start appreciating the full spectrum of what you bring to the world. You'll also learn how to dismantle any distorted or outdated self-concepts you may hold.

In the last chapter, you'll put together all you've learned. You'll review the secret terms of your implicit EIP relationship contract and see if you're ready to put your relationship on a more equal footing. Your ultimate recovery goal is to build a loyal, committed relationship to your own inner self and well-being. You'll also learn how to transform your EI relationship into the best it can be, without sacrificing your integrity or blaming them.

Finally, in the epilogue, you'll be given a new bill of rights for all adult children of emotionally immature parents. These rights express the book's main ideas and can be used as quick reminders of what you've learned.

My Wish for You

I hope you come away from reading this book feeling understood and empowered to live your life from a new place of self-connection and self-understanding. Your parents gave you life and love, but only of the sort they knew. You can honor them for that but cease to give them unwarranted power over your emotional well-being. Your mission now is for your own growth: to become an individual who is fully engaged with both yourself and other people. It would be my dream come true if you find this book useful in that quest.

Part I

What You've Been Up Against

Dealing with Emotional Immaturity

In the first part of this book, you'll learn how it feels to be involved with emotionally immature (EI) parents, how they got to be that way, their personality characteristics, and why it's hard to have a satisfying, close relationship with them. You'll learn tools and interactional strategies to protect your healthy limits in spite of their emotional distortions and attempts to dominate. You'll understand why it's so important to be loyal to yourself around them and how to resist their urgent demands and emotional coercions.

Chapter 1

Your Emotionally Immature Parent

What It's Like to Be Involved with Them and How They Got to Be That Way

Emotionally immature (EI) parents are both frustrating and demoralizing. It's hard to love an emotionally blocked parent who expects honor and special treatment but tries to control and dismiss you at the same time.

A relationship with an EI parent is characterized by not getting your emotional needs met. They have little interest in experiencing *emotional intimacy* in which two people come to know and understand each other at a deep level. This mutual sharing of deepest feelings creates a satisfying, deep bond that makes the participants precious to each other, but this is not something EI parents feel comfortable doing.

Sometimes you glimpse a fleeting desire in them for real connection, and this keeps you reaching out to them. Unfortunately, the more you reach out, the further they recede, wary of real intimacy. It's like being in a dance with someone who is moving away from you in perfect synchrony to your efforts to get close. Their demands for attention, coupled with wariness about intimacy, create a push-me, pull-me relationship that leaves you unsatisfied and emotionally lonely. You care about your parent, but you can't get close enough to have a real relationship.

Once you understand them, however, your experiences will make perfect sense to you—and so will your emotional loneliness. By comprehending the EI psyche, you will be able to deal with your EI parents—or any emotionally immature person (EIP)—in ways that free you from their *emotional coercions* and create a more genuine relationship based on knowing what you can and can't expect from them.

In this chapter, we'll explore what it's like to be intimately involved with such emotionally ungiving parents. You'll learn about the *emotionally immature relationship system* (EIRS) they use as a substitute for love, and you'll get to see how EI parents probably got to be the way they are.

As part of your discovery process, it's a good idea to keep a journal about what you learn as you go along. Throughout this book, you'll find exercises to help you process what you read about. As you record your self-discoveries—hopefully in a new journal especially for this purpose—you'll be giving yourself vital emotional support and validation, two things that EI parents have in short supply.

The writing process will help you finally put words on previously elusive and undefined experiences. Be sure to take notes on the feelings, memories, and insights that arise as you read. These entries can be about your parents or any EIP you have known. As you record your experiences and realizations, leave a couple of blank lines after each entry for later insights. It will be invaluable to look back later and see where you began. In that spirit, let's look at how you came to be reading this book.

Exercise: Why You Picked Up This Book

Take a moment to think about what attracted you to this book. In your journal—or just on some paper for now—write down what intrigued you when you saw the title. What did you hope you would find out and about whom? How has this person made you feel? How do you wish your relationship with this person were different? If this person is no longer living, how do you wish your relationship could've been?

Now let's examine what it is like to be in a relationship with an EI parent or other EIP and how they make you feel. This can stir up old issues, so—as in any self-discovery process—please be sure to seek out a psychotherapist for extra help and support as needed.

What It's Like Being Involved with Them

EI parents and other EIPs have a recognizable interpersonal style. The following ten experiences describe what to expect in a relationship with them.

1. You Feel Emotionally Lonely Around Them

Growing up with EI parents fosters *emotional loneliness*. Although your parent may have been physically present, emotionally you may have felt left on your own. Although you may feel a family bond to your EI parent, that's very different from an emotionally secure parent-child relationship.

EI parents like to tell their children what to do, but they are uncomfortable with emotional nurturing. EI parents may take good care of you when you're sick, but they don't know what to do with hurt feelings or broken hearts. As a result, they may seem artificial and awkward when trying to soothe a distressed child.

2. Interactions Feel One-Sided and Frustrating

EI parents' self-absorption and limited empathy make interactions with them feel one-sided. It's as if they're imprisoned in their own self-involvement. When you try to share something important to you, they're likely to talk over you, change the subject, start talking about themselves, or dismiss what you're saying. Children of EI parents often know a great deal more about their parents' issues than the parents know about theirs.

Although EI parents require your attention when they're upset, they rarely offer listening or empathy when you're distressed. Instead of sitting with you and letting you get it all out, EI parents typically offer superficial solutions, tell you not to worry, or even get irritated with you for being upset. Their heart feels closed, like there's no place you can go inside them for compassion or comfort.

3. You Feel Coerced and Trapped

EI parents insist you put them first and let them run the show. To this end, they coerce you with shame, guilt, or fear until you do what they want. They can flare into blame and anger if you don't toe the line.

Many people use the word *manipulation* for these kinds of emotional coercions, but I think that word is misleading. These behaviors are more like survival instincts. They do whatever's necessary to feel more in control and protected in the moment, oblivious to what it might cost you.

You can also feel trapped by their superficial style of relating. Because EI parents relate in a superficial, egocentric way, talking with them is often boring. They stick to conversation topics they feel safe with, which quickly become stagnant and repetitious.

4. They Come First, and You Are Secondary

EI parents are extremely self-referential, meaning that everything is always about them. They expect you to accept second place when it comes to their needs. They elevate their own interests to the point that yours feel downgraded. They're not looking for an equal relationship. They want blind allegiance to their need to be considered first.

Without a parent willing to give your emotional needs a high priority, it can leave you feeling insecure. Wondering if a parent will think of you or have your back can make you vulnerable to stress, anxiety, and depression. These are reasonable reactions to a childhood environment in which you couldn't trust a parent to notice your needs or protect you from things that overwhelmed you.

5. They Won't Be Emotionally Intimate or Vulnerable with You

Although they're highly reactive emotionally, EI parents actually avoid their deeper feelings (McCullough et al. 2003). They fear being emotionally exposed and often hide behind a defensive exterior. They even avoid tenderness toward their children because this might make them too vulnerable. They also worry that showing love might undermine their power as parents because power is all they think they've got.

Even though EI parents hide their vulnerable feelings, they can show plenty of intense emotion when they fight with their partner, complain about their problems, blow off steam, or fly into a fury with their kids. When upset, they don't look like they are at all afraid of what they feel. However, these one-sided eruptions of emotion are merely releases of emotional pressures. That's not the same thing as a willingness to be open to real emotional connection.

For this reason, comforting them is hard to do. They want you to feel how upset they are, but they resist the intimacy of real comforting. If you try to make them feel better, they may stiff-arm you away. This poor *receptive capacity* (McCullough 1997) prevents them from taking in any comfort and connection you try to offer.

6. They Communicate Through Emotional Contagion

Instead of talking about their feelings, EI people express themselves nonverbally through *emotional contagion* (Hatfield, Rapson, and Le 2009), coming across your boundaries and getting you as upset as they are. In family systems theory, this absence of healthy boundaries is called *emotional fusion* (Bowen 1985), while in structural family therapy it is called *enmeshment* (Minuchin 1974). This is the process by which EI family members get absorbed into each other's emotions and psychological issues.

Like small children, EI parents want you to intuit what they feel without their saying anything. They feel hurt and angry when you don't guess their needs, expecting you to know what they want. If you protest that they didn't tell you what they wanted, their reaction is, "If you really loved me, you would've known." They expect you to stay constantly attuned to them. It's legitimate for a baby or small child to expect such attention from their parent, but not for a parent to expect that from their child.

7. They Don't Respect Your Boundaries or Individuality

EI parents don't really understand the point of boundaries. They think boundaries imply rejection, meaning you don't care enough about them to give them free access to your life. This is why they act incredulous, offended, or hurt if you ask them to respect your privacy. They feel loved only when you let them interrupt you any time. EI parents seek dominant and privileged roles in which they don't have to respect others' boundaries.

EI parents also don't respect your individuality because they don't see the need for it. Family and roles are sacrosanct to them, and they don't understand why you should want space or an individual identity apart from them. They don't understand why you can't just be like them, think like them, and have the same beliefs and values. You are their child and, therefore, belong to them. Even when you're grown, they expect you to remain their compliant child or—if you insist on your own life—at least always follow their advice.

8. You Do the Emotional Work in the Relationship

Emotional work (Fraad 2008) is the effort you make to emotionally adapt to other people's needs. Emotional work can be easy—such as being polite and pleasant—or deeply complicated, such as trying hard to say the right thing to your distraught teenager. Emotional work is comprised of empathy, common sense, awareness of motives, and anticipating how someone is likely to respond to your actions.

When things go wrong in a relationship, the need for emotional work skyrockets. Apologizing, seeking reconciliation, and making amends are among the strenuous emotional labors that sustain healthy long-term relationships. But because EI parents lack interest in relationship repairs, reconnection efforts may fall to you.

Instead of amends or apologies, EI parents often make things worse by projecting blame, accusing others, and disowning responsibility for their behavior. In a situation where it would seem easier just to go ahead and apologize, EI parents can be adamant that it was something you did—or failed to do—that warranted their hurtful behavior. If only you had known better and done what they asked, this problem never would've occurred.

9. You Lose Your Emotional Autonomy and Mental Freedom

Because EI parents see you as an extension of themselves, they disregard your inner world of thoughts and feelings. Instead, they claim the sole right to judge your feelings as either sensible or unwarranted. They don't respect your *emotional autonomy*, your freedom and right to have your own feelings.

Because your thoughts should reflect theirs, they react with shock and disapproval if you have ideas that offend them. You are not free to consider certain things even in the privacy of your own mind. ("Don't even think about it!") Your thoughts and feelings are filtered through their comfort level as either *good* or *bad*.

10. They Can Be Killjoys and Even Sadistic

EI parents can be awful killjoys, both to their children and to other people. They rarely resonate with others' feelings, so they don't take pleasure in other people's happiness. Instead of enjoying their child's accomplishments, EI parents can react in ways that take the shine off the child's pride. They also are famous for deflating their children's dreams by reminding them about depressing realities of adult life.

For instance, as a teenager, Martin proudly told his father that he had made fifty dollars on his first music gig. His father's immediate reaction was to point out that nobody can support a family on that kind of wage. Lacking empathy, his father completely missed the emotional point.

Sadism goes beyond being a killjoy and takes actual pleasure in inflicting pain, humiliation, or forced restraint on a living being. Sadism is also a way of claiming the role as the most powerful and important person in the relationship. Sadistic EI parents enjoy making their child suffer, whether by physical or psychological means. Physical abuse is obviously sadistic, but hidden sadism is often expressed in "teasing" and "joking around."

For instance, when Emily introduced her fiancé to her family, her physically abusive father "joked" that the young man should throw her out if she ever got too mouthy. Her mother and sisters chimed in to "tease" Emily, and they laughed at Emily's excruciating embarrassment.

Sadistic parents like it when their child feels powerless. They secretly enjoy making their children feel desperate by giving them extreme physical punishments, refusing to interact with them for long periods of time, handing down unfathomably long restrictions, or making them feel trapped. For instance, when Bruce was a little boy, his father would squeeze him tightly on his lap and refuse to let him down. If Bruce started to squirm or cry, his father would send him to his room and beat him with a belt. Later his father would apologize but explain that Bruce brought it on himself by being so "bad."

In the next section, we'll look at how EI parents affect other people's emotions and self-worth. Their relational style has an immediate subconscious impact on your emotions and self-esteem. How they react to you can make you feel bad or good about yourself, depending on whether they want to control you or get you on their side.

The Emotionally Immature Relationship System (EIRS)

Emotionally immature people don't regulate their self-esteem and emotional stability well on their own. They need others to keep them on an even keel by treating them just so. To accomplish this, they act in ways that make other people feel responsible for keeping them happy. They do this through complex, extremely subtle cues that influence others to feel certain ways. I call this the *emotionally immature relationship system* (EIRS).

This EIRS draws you into being more attentive to the EI parent's emotional state than to your own self. Under the influence of this relationship system, you attune to the EI parent's emotional needs instead of listening to what your instincts are telling you. It feels imperative to pacify the EI parent's moods at all costs. You find yourself putting their needs and feelings above your own emotional health. This unhealthy overconcern with keeping them calm focuses you on them and their reactions, to the point where you can become obsessed with the status of their moods. Once this happens, they have done an *emotional takeover* on you. An emotional takeover is when their emotional state has become the center of your attention.

In the early stages of human life, the EIRS is normal. The EIRS is a necessary emotional arrangement between babies and their caretakers. To survive and grow, babies require loving adults to be attuned to their needs and soothe them when they're upset. A baby's cries distress normal parents to the point where they will do anything to calm their child. With sensitive parents, the child's distress instantly becomes the parents' distress, and they will be just as concerned about the child's emotional state as the child's physical comfort (Ainsworth, Bell, and Strayton 1974; Schore 2012). This crucial emotional assistance is critical during infancy and toddlerhood.

With normal children, the need for constant engagement and soothing lessens as they mature. But for EI parents, their emotional self-regulation didn't fully develop as they grew up. Unable to modulate their own emotions and disappointments, they still expect others to make them feel better immediately by knowing just how they want to be treated. If they aren't made the priority, they threaten to fall apart. Like little children, they need a lot of attention, compliance, and positive feedback to keep them stable. Unlike children, however, they don't grow from the attention. Their early emotional wounds and deprivations promote psychological defenses that keep them stuck in the same old defensive patterns no matter how much nurturing they get.

How Their EIRS Affects You

You probably won't notice when you first are getting caught up in someone's EIRS. The emotional contagion (Hatfield, Rapson, and Le 2009) in this interpersonal system is so instantly compelling, you are in it before you know it. That's why understanding their relationship pressure up front is so important for protecting your boundaries, emotional autonomy, and sense of self-worth. You have to be alert and prepared in order for it not to take you over.

You Feel Responsible for Their Feelings

Think of the EIRS as a kind of spell they put on you, convincing you that *their* happiness is *your* responsibility. You likewise are held accountable for their anger and bad moods, as though you should've prevented their discomfort in the first place.

When EIPs and EI parents get upset, their distress worms its way into your mind and takes center stage. You worry obsessively about how to make things right with them, and you can't get what they said or did out of your mind. Even while you are doing other things or perhaps trying to sleep at night, their discomfort hovers over you, prompting constant thoughts like, *What did I do wrong? What can I do to make it better?* or *Have I done enough to help them?*

As you are infiltrated by their unhappiness, you feel like it's up to you to make everything all right. Their EIRS has pulled you into their experience to the point that their pain is your pain. You lose sight of your own feelings and needs. Once their EIRS takes you over emotionally, their problem feels like *your* problem, even if rationally you know better.

─────John's Story─────

John's elderly mother lived in a nice retirement community, but she frequently called him with problems that the facility's staff could easily fix. She always sounded so urgent that John felt he had to drop everything and hurry over there to help. Actually, she didn't need a handyman; she just needed to know she could have access to her son at any time. Even though John knew his mother wasn't as desperate as she seemed, he found himself unable to rest when she sounded upset.

———Frank's Story———

Frank's divorced father, Robert, frequently called him in the middle of the night after drinking heavily. Robert often locked himself out of his apartment and called Frank to come get him. When Robert became ill, he asked Frank to stay at the hospital with him "because I don't have anyone else." Frank couldn't say no because his father sounded so pitiful. Frank's family and work began to suffer as he became increasingly preoccupied with Robert's problems. Frank had become so identified with Robert's troubles that it didn't occur to him that his father might have some responsibility to get himself straight.

Healthy and mature people certainly need help sometimes too. But they go about it differently. When they ask for help, they consider the other person's circumstances. They leave room for the other person to say no. They don't expect you to drop everything and attend to them, and they are appreciative when you do help them. Conversely, EI parents impose emotional pressure, then imply that you don't really care about them if you say no.

You Feel Exhausted and Apprehensive

Getting caught up in someone's EIRS is exhausting because you are doing so much emotional work on their behalf. In relationships with any EIPs or parents, you will expend much more psychological energy on them than you would with other people.

Also, you're always waiting for the other shoe to drop because you're chronically apprehensive about what their next emergency is going to be. Once their EIRS gets under your skin, the threat of their next mood shift looms over you and keeps you on red alert. This involuntary, nonstop monitoring of their mood is incredibly draining.

Mature people know you can't be available at all times. They are sensitive to your circumstances and respect your limits.

You Feel You Can't Say No

EI parents dump their problems on you in such an agitated, victimized way that it seems you can't refuse. Before you realize it, your feelings are unimportant, and your mission becomes their stabilization. Once this happens, you have forfeited your emotional autonomy—your freedom to honor and follow what *you* feel.

EI parents pressure you into whatever role best serves their emotional needs. For instance, when they feel overwhelmed, you find yourself stepping in to fix things. If they feel wronged, you feel vengeful on their behalf. If they feel lonely or unimportant, you might find yourself expressing a level of love and loyalty beyond what you actually feel. Such is the power of the EIRS.

EI parents don't just act wounded or abandoned if you can't help. They'll quickly become angry or outraged if you don't comply. First they play on your sympathies, then they threaten you with their displeasure. If you don't jump to make them feel better right away, they act insulted and accuse you of being heartless. You are branded a selfish, unreliable person for anything less than making their issues your most important concern.

In a family, an EI parent's EIRS creates an atmosphere of emotional totalitarianism. All eyes are on that parent's moods and needs because if the child doesn't soothe the parent's distress, the parent might escalate and go to pieces. This usually brings the child back into line because nothing is more horrifying to a child than to witness a grown parent coming apart emotionally. The same could be said of one's mate, friend, or boss.

You Feel Defeated When You Try to Solve Their Problems

Even though they complain to you, EI parents are usually not receptive to any ideas about solving their problems. For them, this is not a two-way interaction. They might even act affronted or offended if you offer suggestions. They get impatient with your problem-solving, and often say, "Yes, but..." because clearly you don't appreciate how impossible their situation is. In fact, they are a little indignant that you would think it could be so simply solved. Don't you see how thorny, complicated, and special their problem is? Can't you just be on their side?

EI parents rarely ask politely for help with problems, such as, "Could you help me with this?" or "What steps should I take to fix this situation?" Instead, they infect you with their anxious urgency as though it's your job to take over and make their problems go away. But it won't be over when you solve that first problem; it will be just beginning.

Your assistance won't satisfy them for long. One helpful act will never be enough because their primary goal is to hold on to your attention and concern as long as possible. They don't want guidance; they want *you*. Their continuing, insoluble problems are the perfect means to that end. Once you start solving their problems, their issues will proliferate faster than a hydra's heads. Problems are the currency that keeps you locked into their EIRS.

You Feel Accused of Letting Them Down

It's likely that EI parents unconsciously project their own unsatisfying early mother-child relationship onto their relationship with you. This may be why they often act like you don't love or care about them enough. You may feel blamed as if you had reenacted their parent's betrayal from a childhood trauma. You might feel like a villain from an old family story that has little to do with who you are.

——————Jill's Story——————

Jill's mother, Claire, became distraught when Jill went ahead on a long-planned trip a week after Claire had had a minor car accident that left her unhurt. She secretly hoped Jill would cancel her trip, but when she didn't, Claire felt wounded. "I thought you *loved* me," Claire cried to Jill, feeling as bereft as she probably did when her own mother sent her away to live with grandparents in her early childhood. As Claire unconsciously projected her early abandonment trauma onto her relationship with her adult daughter, she treated Jill as if she were the abandoning mother from her own deprived childhood.

You Have Overly Intense Emotional Reactions to Them

EI parents can draw you into reacting to them with unusual emotional intensity. That's because they offload their unpleasant emotional states by acting in ways that stir up the same emotions in you. They pretend they don't have such emotions, but actually they project them onto you to be contained and processed so that it seems you're the one having the feeling. For instance, a passive-aggressive EIP might make you furious while they remain unaware of the extent of their own anger. This unconscious way of getting rid of disturbing emotion by making others feel it is called *projective identification* (Ogden 1982). As with children, you end up saddled with their difficult, disowned emotions. This happens so fast—and so below the level of normal consciousness—that you find yourself in the middle of these feelings before you know it. It's an extraordinary psychological phenomenon, whereby EIPs cope with unconscious, disowned emotion by arousing it in another person.

Therefore, when you get entangled in anyone's EIRS, it's always a good idea to ask yourself: *Whose feeling is this?* If your reactions seem overly intense, oddly absent, or unlike yourself, it's possible that the EIP has induced certain feelings in you for you to handle instead. With EIPs, get some perspective on your reactions by asking yourself: *Is this coming from me or them?* It's important to step back and ask this because if you can figure out that this transfer has occurred, it will free you from taking a false responsibility for that emotion.

How EI Parents Got to Be This Way

EI parents may have had difficult childhoods of their own, including histories of abuse and emotional deprivation. Earlier generations lacked parenting classes, psychotherapy, school counselors, and cultural norms that protected the rights of children. Back then, physical punishment, emotional abuse, and shaming were commonplace disciplinary tools. If EI parents suffered neglected or traumatic childhoods, they will show signs of that by being overly preoccupied with their immediate needs, like someone who is always checking an unhealed wound. Following are some questions for you to consider about your parents' upbringing.

Did they grow up without a deep enough connection? EI parents lack the calm depth that emotionally nourished people have. They don't show the security and deep self-acceptance that come from connecting with a sensitive caretaker in childhood. Perhaps it was their own lack of childhood connection that makes them insist on absolute loyalty and sacrifice from their children. They behave as if they are terrified that they don't really matter.

Without a secure attachment in childhood, EI parents can grow up feeling defensive, wary of their deeper feelings, and unable to forge warm connections with their children. This limits them to relating at a superficial level. What they never got in love and security they may try to make up for later through controlling others.

Could they have internalized unresolved family traumas? Many of my clients reported family histories of multigenerational traumas, such as losses, abandonments, deprivation, abuse, addictions, financial disasters, health crises, or disruptive moves. Unfortunately, family traumas tend to be passed down and reenacted (Van der Kolk 2014) between parent and child, creating generations of emotional suffering and immaturity until someone in the family finally stops and consciously processes their painful feelings (Wolynn 2016).

Were they allowed to develop a sense of self? In past generations, children were to be seen and not heard. It's likely that in such a social climate, EI parents were not helped to develop enough emotional awareness to feel a sense of self.

This is serious because a sense of self is the emotional basis for our sense of who we are (Jung 1959; Kohut 1971; Schwartz 1995). Without this sense of self, we don't feel whole, worthy, or genuinely self-confident and must depend upon external definers for identity. Many EI parents disregarded or repressed their inner experiences to the point where external referencing became their only source of security. Without a genuine sense of self-worth and identity, a person has to wrest that from the outside world and other people.

Developing a sense of self is also necessary for the *self-awareness* and *self-reflection* that allow us to observe ourselves and how our behavior affects other people. Without a sense of self fostered in childhood, people can't self-reflect and therefore have no way to grow and change psychologically. Instead, they are limited to blaming others and expecting others to change first.

Highlights to Remember

Now you can see what you've been up against with an EI parent. You learned about their emotionally immature relationship system (EIRS) and how it makes you feel responsible for their self-esteem and emotional stability. You saw how they monopolize interactions with their own issues, and tell you how you should think and feel. We explored how EI parents' childhoods might've influenced their personality and behaviors and how your parents may carry unresolved family traumas of their own. Now you are in an excellent position to question these family dynamics and take care of your own development in spite of anyone's emotional coercions.

Chapter 2

Understanding Emotionally Immature Parents

Their Personality Traits and Emotional Takeovers

EI parents and EIPs approach life and relationships in a me-first way that makes others feel disregarded. But once you understand their personality traits, you won't take their rejections so personally, and you won't feel as pressured by their emotional needs. So before we go any further, let's assess the EI characteristics of your parent.

In your journal, note which of the following statements describe one or both of your parents (Gibson 2015).

1. My parent often overreacted to relatively minor things.

2. My parent didn't express much empathy or awareness of my feelings.

3. When it came to deeper feelings and emotional closeness, my parent seemed uncomfortable and didn't go there.

4. My parent was often irritated by individual differences or different points of view.

5. When I was growing up, my parent used me as a confidant but wasn't a confidant for me.

6. My parent often said and did things without thinking about people's feelings.

7. I didn't get much attention or sympathy from my parent, except maybe when I was really sick.

8. My parent was inconsistent—sometimes wise, sometimes unreasonable.

9. Conversations mostly centered on my parent's interests.

10. If I became upset, my parent either said something superficial and unhelpful or got angry and sarcastic.

11. Even polite disagreement could make my parent very defensive.

12. It was deflating to tell my parent about my successes because it didn't seem to matter.

13. I frequently felt guilty for not doing enough or not caring enough for them.

14. Facts and logic were no match for my parent's opinions.

15. My parent wasn't self-reflective and rarely looked at their part in a problem.

16. My parent tended to be a black-and-white thinker, unreceptive to new ideas.

Because all these behaviors are typical of EI personalities, even checking a few of these traits strongly suggests the presence of emotional immaturity.

Types of EI Parents

There is a broad spectrum of emotional immaturity, from the very mild to the frankly psychopathological. Being emotionally immature isn't the same thing as being mentally ill, but many mentally ill people are also emotionally immature. Emotional immaturity is a broader concept than a clinical diagnosis and therefore is more useful and less pathologizing. It can underlie many psychological problems, especially personality disorders such as narcissistic, histrionic, borderline, antisocial, or paranoid personalities, among others. What all EIPs have in common are self-preoccupation, low empathy, a need to be most important, little respect for individual differences, and difficulties with emotional intimacy.

EI parents can be *extraverted* or *introverted*. Extraverted EI parents demand attention and interaction, making their egocentrism easier to spot. Introverted EI parents may seem less showy, but underneath, they are just as self-involved as the noisier ones. They too show limited empathy or interest in your experiences and offer a one-sided relationship that keeps the focus on them, albeit in a quieter way.

Let's now look at the four basic types of EI parents (Gibson 2015):

1. *Emotional* parents are dominated by feelings and can become extremely reactive and overwhelmed by anything that surprises or upsets them. Their moods are highly unstable, and they can be frighteningly volatile. Small things can be like the end of the world, and they tend to see others as either saviors or abandoners, depending on whether their wishes are being met.

2. *Driven* parents are super goal-achieving and constantly busy. They are constantly moving forward, focused on improvements, and trying to perfect everything, including other people. They run their families like deadline projects but have little sensitivity to their children's emotional needs.

3. *Passive* parents are the nicer parents, letting their mate be the bad guy. They appear to enjoy their children but lack deeper empathy and won't step in to protect them. While they seem more loving, they will acquiesce to the more dominant parent, even to the point of overlooking abuse and neglect.

4. *Rejecting* parents aren't interested in relationships. They avoid interaction and expect the family to center around their needs, not their kids. They don't tolerate other people's needs and want

to be left alone to do their own thing. There is little engagement, and they can become furious and even abusive if things don't go their way.

Next, we'll learn how to identify the personality characteristics that reveal emotional immaturity.

How They Reveal Their Emotional Immaturity

In addition to the relationship problems we saw in chapter 1, EI parents have particular psychological characteristics. Now, we'll examine the personality traits and behaviors that are classic indicators of emotional immaturity in EI parents, as well as in EIPs in general.

How EI Parents Approach Life

EI parents have a very self-absorbed orientation to life and deal with other people in me-first ways.

EI Parents Are Fundamentally Fearful and Insecure

As we saw in the last chapter, many EI parents have probably suffered emotional deprivation, abuse, or trauma in their childhoods. At the deepest level, they act like they don't feel truly loved, making them fearful of losing status and ceasing to matter. Anxieties about abandonment and fears of being shamefully inadequate fuel their discomfort. With these deep fears about being unlovable, they must control others in order to feel safer.

They Need to Dominate and Control

Emotional, driven, and rejecting EI parents try to control others, while passive EI parents go along with whatever the dominant one does. All types do whatever it takes to give them a sense of security.

EI parents dominate you most effectively by taking advantage of your emotions. They influence your behavior by treating you in ways that induce fear, shame, guilt, or self-doubt. Once EI parents elicit these negative emotional states, you're the one with the problem, not them. They feel better once you're the "bad" one, but only temporarily because nothing makes them feel secure for long.

To justify being in charge, EI parents treat others as lacking in judgment and competence. This gives them license to tell you what to do and how to be. Such overcontrol can be especially destructive to a child's sense of efficacy and confidence. EI parents also hold their children back by foreseeing dire happenings if the parent's advice isn't followed.

Because their focus is on gaining control, EI parents lack the genuine warmth of more mature people. They may act warmly, but it feels staged. Instead of real warmth and openness, EIPs are limited to charm and charisma. They've got their eye on interpersonal dominance, not relational connection.

They Define Themselves and Others by Roles

Roles are central to an EI parent's security and self-identity. They certainly expect others to stay in clear-cut roles. They categorize people into either dominant or submissive roles because equal relationships make them uneasy, uncertain who's really in charge.

EI parents often use their parental role to take liberties with your boundaries. In this way, they keep you in a position they are comfortable with. They are likely to disallow any individuality that could threaten your family role.

They Are Egocentric, Not Self-Reflective

EI parents put their desires first. They assume they are entitled to what they want and rarely look at themselves objectively. Because their own inner world is unexamined, they seldom question their motives or reactions. For instance, they would rarely wonder whether they were causing any of their own hardships.

Personal *growth* is not a concept they relate to, and they are usually derisive of it. Lacking self-reflection, they're not interested in *learning* about themselves or *improving* their relationships, other than how they can get more of what they want. In general, growth is threatening to them because it means unpredictable change and more insecurity.

Because they aren't self-reflective, EI parents have poor filters and say things without thinking. They can leave people stunned by their inappropriate comments. If confronted with their insensitivity, they might say things like, "I was only saying what I thought," as if speaking all your thoughts out loud were normal behavior.

They Blame Others and Excuse Themselves

Many EI parents are mistrustful, seeing the world as against them. It often seems to them that other people are making them unhappy for no good reason. Their mistrust makes them blame others when things go wrong, making their relationships highly conflictual and unstable. They excuse themselves from responsibility because their brittle self-esteem can't take criticism. Their self-esteem is based on whether or not things have gone their way, feeling inflated if they do and desperate if they don't.

They Are Impulsive and Don't Tolerate Stress

EI parents don't handle stress well. They have a hard time waiting and often impatiently rush their children and other people. Their low tolerance for stress makes them feel that all is lost when life hits a bump in the road. They don't know how to soothe themselves other than to make problems go away as quickly as possible. They grab at the next action that makes them feel better. Sometimes this works; sometimes it doesn't. Often the solution they hit upon makes things worse. They are known for doing impulsive things that backfire on them. Their attempts to avoid stress usually end up causing much more stress.

How They Deal with Reality

Instead of adapting to reality, EI parents try to remake reality. Although reality is a blooming, buzzing, evolving mass of stimulation, EIPs cope by oversimplifying reality into streamlined parts that make sense and seem manageable to them.

They Use Coping Mechanisms That Resist Reality

George Vaillant (1977) is a researcher who became famous for his thirty-year participation in Harvard's Grant Study of Adult Development, a research project that followed men's lives for decades to identify the factors that correlated with health, successful functioning, and happiness. He developed a rating scale to assess how successfully and adaptively a person deals with life, a kind of index of emotional maturity. Vaillant concluded that we adapt best to life when we are aware of our own feelings and motives and can assess reality objectively.

Adaptive, emotionally mature people have balanced lives and emotionally satisfying relationships. They can comfortably relate to the inner experiences of themselves and others. They accept reality on its own terms, adapting to it and mostly not fighting it. Their coping mechanisms are flexible, and instead of trying to rigidly control everything, they look for the most adaptive, least stressful solution that takes all factors into account. To get through tough times, they might use humor, creativity, deliberate suppression of unhelpful thoughts, and altruism.

In contrast, the most immature EIPs try to alter reality by denying, dismissing, or distorting facts they don't like. At the lowest level of maladaptive coping mechanisms, a person might lose touch with consensual reality and become psychotic.

Some EIPs can be realistic about objective reality, but can't deal with feelings. They use defenses like rationalizing, intellectualizing, and minimizing to dodge unpleasant emotions or keep them at a distance. They might also indulge substance abuse or other forms of acting out to hide from painful feelings, even though their awareness of factual reality may be intact.

Reality Is Determined by Their Emotions

Because EIPs and EI parents approach life emotionally rather than thoughtfully (Bowen 1985), they define reality based on how it *feels* to them. Perceiving reality as identical to the way one feels at the moment is called *affective realism* (Barrett 2017; Clore and Huntsinger 2007). We all do this—when we feel good, things look good—but EIPs take this to an extreme. The way it *feels* to them is the way it *is*.

For example, Darcy's mother used to make pronouncements about things that simply were not true, just because they occurred to her. Darcy wasn't sure why this so infuriated her, but then she realized that it was emblematic of her mother's pathological egocentricity: everything and everybody should be what she thought they should be.

They Deny and Dismiss the Reality of Others' Feelings

EI parents are thin-skinned themselves, but they are often insensitive to other people's feelings. Because of their low empathy, they frequently respond in ways that other people find insensitive or hurtful. This lack of emotional resonance with others lowers their emotional intelligence (Goleman 1995), making it harder to get along with people.

Their Intense Emotions Oversimplify Reality

EIPs and EI parents have intense, all-or-nothing emotions, like the unmodulated feelings of little children. They oversimplify people and situations into categories of all good or all bad. Their black-and-white thinking prevents them from experiencing conflicting emotions at the same time, so there is little balancing or tempering of their emotions. This is a serious problem because blended, nuanced emotions are necessary for a richer, truer perception of our multifaceted reality. Emotional maturity allows you to experience a simultaneous mixture of emotions, such as feeling sad yet grateful or angry but cautious. It is only through our own emotional complexity that we can grasp the subtler emotions of other people, as well as the full implications of reality.

They Disregard Reality's Time Sequence

Appreciating how life events are hooked together on a timeline is crucial to understanding how cause and effect works. However, EIPs live in the immediate emotional moment and can be oblivious to the chain of causation over time. Instead of seeing reality as a timeline, EIPs experience events as isolated blips unrelated to each other. This makes it hard for them to anticipate the future or to learn from errors. Ignoring time's sequential reality lets them say and do the most dumbfounding things because they don't feel the need to be logically consistent with their past statements or actions. For instance, they may be blithely oblivious to how their recent behavior has made them unwelcome. They can't see why things shouldn't go back to normal when they are ready to interact again.

Instead of analyzing their mistakes, they think, *That was then; this is now.* They are famous for their philosophy of "moving on" and "getting over it" and other forms of not processing the lessons of the past. They don't connect the dots to see the overall trajectory of their lives. Therefore, they don't notice when they are repeating past mistakes, nor can they steer themselves toward a different future.

The future isn't a real consideration for them, so they feel free to deceive others, burn bridges, or create enemies. In seeking immediate gratifications, their future is left to take care of itself, often with predictably negative results.

Lack of time sequence awareness also makes lying seem like a reasonable solution. They never seem to realize that past actions or lying will likely catch up with them. They concoct something that gets them off the hook but don't realize others will be suspicious due to past lies.

It can be maddening to try to get EIPs to take responsibility for their past behavior. Because their memories are not meaningfully connected to the present, they don't understand why things from the past should be such a concern now. It's over: why haven't you moved on like they did? They simply don't understand the persistence of cause and effect, especially when other people's feelings are involved.

How They Think

In his study mentioned above, George Vaillant (1977) noted that maturity in coping isn't determined by a person's level of education or social standing. Emotional maturity is much deeper than intellectual ability or conventional success. EIPs and EI parents tend to show certain characteristics of thought, especially in the world of relationships and emotions.

Their Intelligence Doesn't Extend to the World of Feelings

Being emotionally immature doesn't necessarily affect a person's raw intelligence. EIPs can be plenty intelligent as long as there is nothing emotional to unsettle them. Some can be highly intelligent and good at theoretical concepts, working well with abstract ideas or business models. As long as issues are safely cognitive or data-based, they can address the past and future, such as budgets, spreadsheet analyses, and retirement planning. But when it comes to emotionally arousing situations, like relationships or temptations, or subtle empathies, such as sensitivity or tact, they stop paying attention to cause and effect.

Their Thoughts About Life Are Simplistic, Literal, and Rigid

The immature personality structure of EIPs results in oversimplified, black-and-white thinking and rigid moral categories of all good or all bad (Kernberg 1985). The complexity of nuanced or ambiguous situations is boiled down to simplistic judgments that disregard crucial elements. EIPs' thinking tends to be literal, based on a few favorite concepts and well-worn metaphors. They dislike the uncertainty of an evolving reality, so they can irrationally defend what is familiar. Abhorring complexity, they will cast off facts in order to jump to a quick conclusion that agrees with their preconceptions.

Sometimes people mistake the EIP's oversimplifications for wisdom. EIPs and EI parents are famous for making statements that sound catchy and decisive. Thanks to their self-involvement, they deliver these pronouncements with authority. However, if you examine their words closely, they have a trite quality that isn't giving you anything new. This is different from a mature person's wisdom, in which they say things that feed your mind the longer you think about them.

EIPs' mental rigidity makes them sticklers for rules and authoritarian values. They love the feeling of being in control so much that they will arbitrarily make up rules just to have a rule. They stubbornly uphold rules even when situations are so complex that hard-and-fast rules fly in the face of good sense.

However, EIPs' egocentrism also means that they will break the same rules for their own gain. This is why some EIPs can commit such egregious moral misconduct within an otherwise rule-bound culture: if there wasn't a specific rule about that specific behavior on the books, they might do it. EIPs are famous for behaviors that are *so* wrong that no one would've thought to make an explicit rule against it.

EIPs get increasingly single-minded and stubborn as situations become more complicated or stressful. Their one-track mind prevents them from taking individual differences or unanticipated consequences into account. Proud of being unyielding, they call their judgmental rigidity "moral fortitude" or "having a backbone."

———Frieda's Story———

Frieda's EI father was furious when she got engaged to a man from another race. Her father had zero interest in seeing her side of things because she had broken one of his rules. When he couldn't intimidate Frieda into changing her mind, he disowned her. After Frieda left, she felt like a ghost because no one was allowed to welcome her as a family member.

They Become Obsessive

Like Frieda's father, when EIPs or EI parents feel hurt, embarrassed, or like their authority is disrespected, they get stuck in obsessive anger. They see the world as made up of good guys and bad guys, and they dwell obsessively on anyone who they think has wronged them. They lack the mental flexibility or emotional willingness to see things another way.

They Use Superficial Logic to Shut Down Feelings

Instead of offering empathy, EIPs inappropriately apply logic to minimize other people's problems. EIPs get highly upset about their *own* troubles, but they oversimplify your problems and ignore deeper emotional factors. They typically offer platitudes instead of considering your unique dilemma. In their mind, your problems should yield to their simplistic, overly rational advice. When empathy is required, pure logic is an emotionally inappropriate response.

EI parents often use inappropriate logic when their child comes to them for comforting by explaining why they shouldn't let things get to them. They like to suggest clever things children should've said to the person who hurt them ("Well, you should've told him...!"). They tell the child not to be upset, to rise above the distress, and to just stop worrying about it. Of course, this is impossible. What the child really needs is a listening, empathic parent to help them process their distress until they get a handle on it.

When children make mistakes, EI parents also use logic inappropriately by making it seem that the child should've avoided the mistake in the first place. They promote the unrealistic logic that if everyone just thought ahead far enough, there need never be a mistake. For such children, they learn that not only should they feel bad for making a mistake, but they are inadequate as well.

Now that you have a good understanding of your EI parent's personality characteristics and behaviors, let's see how they make you feel bad in order to control you. They use your feelings against you so you feel responsible for supporting their emotional security, stability, and self-esteem. Here's how they dominate you through emotional coercions.

EIPs' Emotional Coercions and Takeover Tactics

Emotional coercion occurs when an EIP controls you by inducing fear, guilt, shame, and self-doubt. I know it's popular to say that nobody can *make* you feel anything, but for most of us that simply isn't true. In fact, EIPs are masters at getting you to feel things that are to their advantage. Children can certainly be made to feel things by powerful adults upon whom they are dependent, and the same goes for us in adulthood whenever there is a power imbalance between people. The achievable goal is not to pretend that you're immune to their influence, but to catch it early and quickly separate yourself from their attempted domination.

Ultimately, as you become skilled at spotting and refusing emotional takeovers, you may no longer be vulnerable to anyone's attempts to make you feel anything. But in the meantime, let's work on getting free from emotional coercions when they occur.

Next, we will look at how EIPs arouse toxic feelings that make you willing to give in and let them take you over.

Self-Doubt Undermines Your Autonomy and Self-Worth

EI parents punish you by withdrawing emotional connection if you express thoughts or feelings they don't like. The fear of this alienation makes you doubt yourself and creates uncertainty about your thoughts and feelings.

Once you are taught to doubt yourself, you start looking to others for direction, trusting other people's perspective over your own. Instead of knowing what you really think and feel, you become preoccupied with just being accepted. Ambivalence undermines your confidence, and you lose contact with your gut feelings and intuitions. You realize that self-doubt brings parental acceptance, while feeling autonomous causes tension. If you want to be accepted and loved by an EI parent, it helps not to be too sure of yourself.

But when you doubt your deeper instincts, you lose clarity of mind. Your thoughts are clouded by polluted waters of self-doubt and fears of rejection. It gets harder and harder to think clearly in the face of their coercive tactics.

We tend to give in to emotional coercions because it's too painful to face that we hate what our parents are doing to us. But hate is just a signal that we are being controlled, and none of us likes to be guilted or held hostage by someone's mood. Your unavoidable emotional reactions may make you worry that you aren't being good or loving enough. But as you doubt your goodness and self-worth, the further you fall under their influence.

Fear Makes You Easier to Control

Fear is perhaps the EIP's simplest, most straightforward tactic for emotional takeovers in which they push you into a psychological state that makes you tractable. EIPs and EI parents are geniuses when it comes to instilling fear and making you feel unsafe. Whether it's a violent outburst or an emotional meltdown, EIPs instinctively use whatever will scare you into the kind of behavior they want. Once you feel afraid, you're much more willing to put them first.

Physical abuse is the biggest fear tactic. Physical fears go deep and must be consciously worked at in order to unlearn their effects. But threats of emotional withdrawal, abandonment, or even suicide can be just as damaging.

You Inhibit Yourself

At first you may just be afraid of an EI parent's reactions, but pretty soon you may start to fear your own *feelings*. You start to identify your natural reactions as the problem, as the avoidable cause of conflict with the EIP in the first place. Tragically, you learn to feel anxious as soon as you start to feel anything your parent wouldn't like (Ezriel 1952). Once you tag some of your feelings as dangerous, you inhibit them as soon as they come up, before your EI parent has a chance to react to them. This self-inhibition shows that you have fallen under their emotional control. You no longer need an external threat to shut yourself down. You know what's going to happen, so you just don't go there.

You Often Feel Guilty

Guilt should be a brief corrective signal, not a chronic condition. Its healthy purpose is to prompt apologies in order to keep good relations with others. Guilt should motivate you to apologize, not hate yourself. Mature guilt helps us learn from mistakes, make amends, and try not to do it again.

However, EI parents exploit the coercive potential of guilt. They teach their children to feel horrible about themselves and feel the need to become perfect. Such children are not taught to forgive themselves for mistakes, and they don't learn that there is a way out of guilt by taking responsibility and making amends. EIPs encourage guilty feelings because then you are more attentive and acquiescent to their needs.

EI parents especially make their children feel guilt over not sacrificing themselves enough, and also survivor guilt whenever they have a happier life than their parents.

Guilt for not self-sacrificing. EI parents often ask for more than you can give. But if you ever say no, they act like you don't really love them. As an adult child of EI parents, it can feel like the only way to be a good person is to sacrifice yourself.

————Gina's Story————

One day Gina's elderly parents informed her they were planning to move closer to her so she could take care of them in their old age. Gina panicked. She had never felt close to her parents, and they were impossible to please. Gina was the eldest child and had always functioned as a surrogate mother to everyone in the family. Gina was also recovering from breast cancer and already felt overwhelmed as a single mother with three teenage boys. She couldn't imagine what it would be like caring for her parents as well. Gina felt that taking on her self-involved parents might be the final health straw. Although she wanted to tell her parents no, she felt too guilty to do so. She asked me, "But don't I have an obligation to my parents?"

My answer was a firm no. Just because her parents wanted Gina to handle things, she wasn't obligated to ignore her situation to give them whatever they wanted. It wasn't Gina's responsibility to endanger her mental and physical health just because her parents preferred her as care-taker. Gina's parents were financially secure and had two other children near them they could turn to, along with a supportive community of friends. Realistically, Gina could recuse herself from her parents' demand without a shred of guilt, but she still felt troubled and obligated.

Gina's parents hadn't considered for a moment how their wishes might place a hardship on Gina. They didn't ask her how she felt about their idea; they just told her they were coming. Gina rightly feared that her EI parents might accuse her of not loving them if she dared say no to them. But this is a false conclusion: setting a limit doesn't mean you don't love somebody. It just means you are claiming the right to think of yourself too.

Fortunately, Gina realized what was happening and was able to see that she was not a bad person because she didn't want to sacrifice her health for her parents' whim. In the end, Gina told them no, and after some hurt feelings and angry withdrawal, they decided to move near her sister instead.

Survivor guilt. Sometimes adult children feel guilty around their EI parents simply because of how much better their lives are going. *Survivor guilt*—feeling guilty for your own good fortune compared to others—can arise if you have EI parents who are not functioning well. EI parents often have multiple problems, both in their work and in their personal relationships. EI parents who stir up survivor guilt might be depressed, mentally ill, addicted, or functioning poorly in adult life. If you have created a life that is happier than theirs, you may actually feel guilty for your success.

Guilt is a conscious feeling that is easily put into words. You can talk about why you feel guilty, citing reasons and describing feelings. Because guilt is familiar and easy to express, sometimes we think we are feeling guilt when we're really experiencing shame.

Feelings of Shame Make You Easy to Dominate

Shame comes from feeling rejected by other people (DeYoung 2015). Shame is much deeper than mere embarrassment because you believe your goodness as a human being is in question. Shame is a powerful, primal experience that says not only have you have *done something wrong* but there's *something wrong with you* as a person. Shame can be so unbearable that the mere threat of it can coerce you into doing whatever an EIP wants. This feeling of being unlovable and unacceptable can lead to what

Jerry Duvinsky (2017) calls a *core shame identity*, a pervasive sense of unworthiness that persists regardless of your positive qualities.

Shaming can make you lose trust in your own thoughts and feelings. EI parents might shame you with phrases like, "Are you crazy? Are you out of your mind?" "How dare you!" "Don't even think that!" "You shouldn't feel that way," or "I never in my life heard such a thing!" Children conclude from these reactions that there is something deeply wrong with them. By embarrassing and shaming their children, EI parents teach them to knuckle under to other people's emotional dominations later in adult relationships.

You might be especially vulnerable to shame if EIPs call you *selfish*. There is no accusation more hurtful to a sensitive person than to be told they don't care about others. EI parents easily bring sensitive children under control by labeling them "selfish." But what EIPs and parents usually mean by selfishness is that you are pausing to think about your needs instead of automatically giving in to their demands.

Shame for Having Needs

A child's dependency often irritates the self-involved EI parent. Preoccupied with their own issues, EI parents can be short-tempered and react to their child's needs as if the child had done something wrong. These parents make their children feel bad for having needs and thereby making the parent's life harder. If you were treated this way as a child, you may still feel ashamed for having problems or needing help.

The Annihilating Sensation of Shame

Patricia DeYoung (2015) describes how devastating it can feel when someone refuses to connect with us at the moment of our greatest emotional need. It's unbearably shaming to have one's pleas for comfort or connection rejected. When a child's efforts to engage a parent fail, the child can feel hopeless, like they are all alone in the world. DeYoung explains that when children feel like they don't matter, their fragile personality structure feels like it's disintegrating—an experience that feels like dying. No wonder that being unresponded to can feel like the end of the world.

In my work with the adult children of EI parents, many of them have remembered deep, annihilating shame experiences of being emotionally rejected by their parents at their moment of greatest need. They describe this awful feeling as "sinking into darkness," "circling a black hole," "being untethered in outer space," "falling into the abyss," or "physically dying." This cessation of existence is what psychological disintegration feels like when an uncaring person witnesses your need but won't respond to you (DeYoung 2015). These experiences are so agonizing that people often banish the memories and try not to recall them.

Such powerless anguish impels children to do something—anything— to make their parent see and respond to them. That's why young children so often have meltdowns over seemingly insignificant things. When their subjective experience isn't recognized or understood by their parent (Stern 2004), their inner cohesion comes apart, and they feel like they're falling into the void. They can't keep themselves together in the absence of a supportive parental attachment (Wallin 2007).

We Don't Recognize Shame as a Feeling

Fear of shame controls us long past childhood because we haven't been taught that it's just an emotion. We don't realize we were treated badly, and instead we think the sensation of shame is a fact of our badness (Duvinsky 2017). As one client said in a moment of insight, "I believe I'm worthless because I *feel* that way." Shame feels like reality because it's such a compelling emotional experience. However, if parents help their children recognize and label shame as just another feeling, they won't end up with such sweeping self-condemnation. However, EI parents have so much buried shame themselves, they can't help their children understand it.

Exercise: Rescue Your Shamed and Fearful Self

Shame and feelings of worthlessness are rooted in fears of not mattering and being abandoned. To combat feelings of shame, Jerry Duvinsky (2017) recommends loosening their grip on you by writing down your fears of shaming and exposing them exactly as they are. My own method is to ask worried or anxious clients to write down the most embarrassing things they could imagine happening. Once you identify what kind of shaming you fear most, push the dread up another notch by asking yourself, "And then what?" until you know you have reached the absolute worst possible outcome of your feared shame. Then just sit with it for a few moments and notice that nothing bad happens; it's just a feeling.

Next, spell out the awful story about yourself that accompanies this shamed state. What is your self-image that goes with the shame? Instead of agreeing that this would be the end of the world, can you feel compassion for how you've been made to feel so terrible about yourself? Now imagine rescuing this shamed inner self and giving it the comfort and acceptance that it needs to feel good about itself again.

When you know that feeling bad about yourself comes from emotional rejection in early childhood, you will see yourself differently. You can understand that feeling unlovable probably came from your parent's incapacity for emotional intimacy and is not a fundamental flaw in yourself. Your needs for emotional connection were normal, not repellant nor unlovable, and would *not* have been overwhelming to an adequately mature parent.

Subtle Shaming Between Peers and Adults

Subtle shaming is frequently used to exert social dominance. These social behaviors can be extremely subtle, such as not responding to your overtures, dismissing your concerns, or implying that you are a bother. These subtle shaming behaviors by another person are often hard to pinpoint because they're not dramatically demeaning or rude. You might think about these incidents for a long time afterward but can't quite put your finger on why you feel so bad. However, once you see subtle shaming for what it is, you will feel better at once. You will see what's happening and stop feeding the EIP's self-esteem by agreeing to feel inferior.

Exercise: Reflect on Your Takeover Experiences

Write in your journal about a time when you felt emotionally coerced by your parent or other EIP. Do you remember a time when they used fear, guilt, shame, or self-doubt to make you do what they wanted? What worked the best on you? What type of emotional coercions are you most vulnerable to? What physical sensations do you get when someone is trying to make you feel bad for their benefit? After thinking about this, write down how you might recognize an emotional coercion in the future and prevent it from taking you over.

Highlights to Remember

In this chapter, you assessed your likelihood of having EI parents and learned about different types of EI parents, as well as the essential personality characteristics of EIPs in general. You also learned about their self-preoccupied approach to life, how they resist reality, and their unique orientation to time. You saw how EI parents use your self-doubt, fear, guilt, and shame to emotionally coerce you into shoring up their self-esteem, emotional stability, and security. These emotional takeovers assert their dominance and undermine your self-confidence—but only as long as you don't see what they're doing.

Chapter 3

Longing for a Relationship with Your EI Parent

Why You Keep Trying

If you have EI parents, you may still long for a closer relationship with them. You may continue to wish they would show more interest in your life. And more than anything, you may still hope that one day they'll love you back in a way that makes you feel seen. Perhaps you've dreamed of finding a way to reach them, if only you could discover the right opening and the right skills. You may have hoped that, as an adult, you could find a way to make them finally be emotionally available.

Unfortunately, the personality defenses and fears of EI parents make it nearly impossible for them to tolerate closeness for long. In this chapter, we'll explore why your hopes for a better relationship with EI parents often leave you feeling disappointed and emotionally lonely.

The Relationship Experiences You Long For

As an adult child of an EI parent, you probably didn't get enough child-hood emotional connection, intimate communication, or parental approval—all the things that make you feel loved by your parents. However, your EI parents might scoff at the idea that you didn't feel loved.

If you confronted them with not loving you, they would be as puzzled as you are. Of course they love you; you're their child. They have no idea they would have to treat you certain ways in order for you to *feel* that.

Feeling love from an EI parent is like trying to experience the mountains by looking at a photograph. You can see the color and shape of them, but you can't experience the crispness of the air, the rustling tree sounds, or the sheer sense of space and grandeur that fills the atmosphere. Like a photograph, you can see your parents, but the sensation of their emotional presence is missing. It's like you're trying to relate to their reflection in a mirror instead of face to face. You can't quite put your finger on it, but you know you're not directly connecting with them.

Now, let's further explore what you've been missing and longing for from your EI parents.

You Long to be Known by Them

We know that children need attention and loving connection, but how exactly does a parent accomplish that? It takes something more than just looking and listening. There has to be active psychological involvement by the parent. A parent can be looking right at a child, and be able to repeat everything the child said, but if the parent isn't also sensitively imagining the child's inner state (Fonagy et al. 2004), the child won't feel a connection. It's not what the parent says; it's how the parent shows interest in the child's unique subjective experience (Stern 2004). When the parent's inner self attunes to the child's inner world, the child feels seen, known, and loved.

Watch young children and parents together, and you'll see how many times the children look to their parents for eye contact and meaningful interaction (Campbell 1977). This isn't just attention-seeking; children get *emotional refueling* from these moments of connection with their parent (Mahler and Pine 1975). Children need their parent's emotional engagement and affection in order to grow stronger, more secure, and eventually more independent. No wonder a parent's love feels so crucial.

Your adult desire for a better relationship with your EI parents partly originates in this inner child that is still looking to be seen and responded to. Unfortunately, trying to connect with an EI parent often comes up against their refusal to engage at a deeper level. The EI parent's nervous avoidance of deep emotions—their affect phobia (McCullough et al. 2003)—makes them pull back from such intimacy.

You Want Better Communication

As an adult, you may have learned good communication skills and how important they are for satisfying relationships. Perhaps you learned to speak up when there's a problem and try to work things out directly with the other person. You might have tried these new skills with your parents. And you may have found that while it is true that effective communication is crucial for good relationships, it only works when the other person is willing to participate.

EI parents are uncomfortable with emotional communication. They are not accustomed to dealing with other people's feelings and don't know what to say. Instead of empathically listening to their children when they're upset or soothing them with affection, EI parents instead often try to comfort their children with treats or activities. Emotional communication doesn't come any easier to them once their child is an adult.

Maybe you just want to have a heart-to-heart with them or talk about how to improve your relationship. You may think you're making a heartfelt attempt at closeness, but they may feel they're being thrown into the deep end of something they can't swim in.

Let's look at your request to talk from your EI parent's viewpoint for a moment. Maybe when your EI parent was a kid, someone wanting to talk to them meant they were in trouble. Telling them you want to talk might make them worry they're about to be blamed for something, increasing their defensiveness. For this reason, it's always best to initiate deeper conversations by first asking for a short amount of their time, say five or ten minutes, and then asking only specific questions or sharing one or two feelings with them at a time. If you keep it short and structured at the beginning, they may be willing to respond later to more open-ended questions.

Exercise: How Did It Go When You Tried to Communicate?

Think about a time when you tried to get your parent to listen and talk with you at a deeper level. How did they respond? How did you feel after opening up to them? Write about this memory in your journal. If their reaction wasn't emotionally satisfying, do you think—given what you've read so far—that the problem may have been their difficulty in relating at a deeper level? Write down your conclusions.

You Long for Their Praise and Approval

Many adult children of EI parents hope that achievements and success will be the magic keys to more of their parent's attention. Even when these adult children create successful lives of their own, they still look for their parent's approval.

Perfectionism and chasing success are ways that some of us might try to win that all-important parental approval and praise. To this end, we may choose life professions to impress our parents or marry mates who seem right off a parental checklist. But it's hard to get praise from self-preoccupied EI parents. They just aren't all that interested in their children's accomplishments, unless it gives the parent bragging rights.

Many of my clients have reported being surprised that their parents boasted about them to a friend, yet never told them directly they were proud of them. This can be confusing, but it makes sense because bragging to others allows EI parents to keep emotional distance while still claiming your accomplishment as social currency. This is emotionally safer for them than looking you in the eye and telling you how pleased they are. EI parents would find such direct, emotionally intimate praise intensely uncomfortable.

EI Behaviors That Prevent Connection

Here are five common EI behaviors that make it hard to have a close relationship with EI parents.

1. They Don't Show Interest

EI parents often seem to lack interest in their children's lives. Due to their low empathy and preoccupation with their own concerns, they seldom show interest in anything beyond what immediately matters to them. These parents might light up while talking about their interests, but act disinterested or distracted when their children share something about their lives.

———Brenda's Story———

Brenda's father, Ben, was a taciturn New Englander. He raised Brenda after her volatile, punitive mother died when Brenda was fifteen. Although Ben mostly kept to himself, he sometimes comforted Brenda after her mother's abusive harangues. Brenda therefore saw him as the more caring parent, even though he otherwise showed little interest in her activities.

Brenda went on to become a well-respected medical researcher. When she was invited to speak about her work at a prestigious international conference, Brenda thought her father would finally be excited and impressed by her accomplishments.

But Ben showed little interest. His tepid responses to Brenda's success crushed her. He seemed to sidestep every effort she made to gain his approval. Even when Ben did come to one of Brenda's award ceremonies, he embarrassed her socially with his gruff and dismissive comments about her work. He could not get out of himself long enough to realize this was not the time to express his opinions.

Ben had very narrow interests, mostly focused on his political beliefs and the state of the economy. Regardless of what Brenda achieved, it seemed unimportant compared to whatever her father was interested in. After each phone call home, Brenda was left with the humiliating feeling that she was begging her father to be proud of her.

2. They Stay Overly Busy

Some EI parents keep distance by staying too busy to stop and connect. Children who grow up with overly busy parents know that their parent's real interests lie elsewhere and that they come in second to the parent's outside pursuits. Such on-the-go parents can be so activity-obsessed or success-driven that their relationships with their children wither. They don't see how they're depriving their child of their presence and attention. Aren't they giving their all, all the time?

Overly busy parents misjudge how much time they are taking away from their families. Such parents may go overboard in workaholism, physical activities, getting an advanced degree, nonstop socializing, or constant volunteering. It's as if these parents can't imagine that such productive activity could be harmful to anyone. If they see signs of problems, they rationalize that the importance of the activity is worth a little sacrifice on everyone's part.

————Katie's Story————

Katie's mother, Bella, was always in the middle of finishing up some activity, such as cleaning the house, fixing dinner, or returning phone calls. When Katie visited, she could tell her mother was antsy to get back to her tasks, using the excuse that she would have time to relax with Katie later. That time never came. Even when Katie had a chance to sit down and talk with her mom, her mother kept one eye on the TV or began doodling in her word game book. When Katie called her mother on it, her mother said, "I'm listening!" but wouldn't stop. Her father was the same way, stealing away at the first opportunity to work in his garage. Her parents' busyness made it impossible for a sustained emotional connection to take root. Their discomfort with intimacy hid behind things that "just have to get done."

Anyone can get caught up in too many activities or duties, such as a demanding job or caretaking responsibilities. But if parents are adequately emotionally sensitive, they will take it seriously if their children complain about not having enough time with them. The more emotionally mature parent will empathize with the child's experience and, if possible, try to create more balance between their activities and their availability to their children.

Of course, sometimes economic realities make it impossible for struggling parents to be available, no matter how emotionally mature they might be. It is a tough time for the whole family when there isn't much choice about how much a parent must work. But if the parent listens to the child's feelings and explains the financial situation, then the child at least knows the separation they experience is for a meaningful reason and not because the parent is more interested in other things.

3. They Show Envy and Jealousy

Some EI parents actually envy their child's success and social attention. Instead of being happy for their child, *envious* parents are more likely to discount and minimize their child's abilities and achievements. These parents lack the maturity to vicariously enjoy another person's good fortune. In their competitive approach to life, a successful offspring threatens to steal their spotlight.

Jealous parents feel left out when their child gets attention from someone else. These parents see the child as stealing attention that should be theirs. While envy is covetous—they want something you have—jealousy is relationship-based. These parents resent that their child is getting special attention that the parents want all to themselves.

——Shonda's Story——

Shonda's mother, Ayana, liked playing the matriarch in her social circle and couldn't stand it when people paid more attention to

Shonda. Even after Shonda was grown, Ayana kept treating Shonda as her child in any social situation. At one family gathering, an uncle came up to greet them. Shonda was a probation officer, and her uncle told her he'd love to hear her opinion of a notorious juvenile crime that had just happened in their neighborhood. Before Shonda could respond, Ayana jumped in with an incredulous tone and said, "*Shonda?* What would *Shonda* know about *that?*" Although Shonda actually knew a lot about that, Ayana couldn't stand for her to have all the attention.

George's Story

George's immature father loved to be the center of attention. When George was a kid and had friends over, his father made George the butt of numerous jokes and put-downs. He drew the other boys into siding with him, disrupting the boys' friendship bond, even though it obviously made George feel bad.

Under these conditions, children of envious and jealous parents might learn it's better to hide their talents or stay out of the spotlight so as not to tempt a put-down from a competitive parent. Due to their parents' envy and jealousy, success can be an ambivalent issue for these adult children.

4. They Get Agitated and Easily Upset

Some EI parents don't keep good emotional connections with anyone because they live in a flurry of crises and unsettled emotion. They can't rest or let things go and are extremely touchy about the smallest things. They are pathologically sensitive to criticism—often seeing it when it's not intended—and never feel like anybody cares about them enough. Sometimes these parents get quite paranoid and feel sure that others are against them for no good reason. They can get so agitated that people around them have a full-time job reassuring them and picking up the pieces when the smallest thing goes wrong. A person who is so consumed with their own anxieties and projections has no room for peaceful, loving connections.

5. They Are Inconsistent and Contradictory

EI parents have a poorly integrated personality structure that leaves them emotionally fragmented and compartmentalized, resulting in very contradictory, inconsistent behaviors. It's hard to have a close adult relationship with them because, like children, they are more an amalgam of reactive moods rather than a consistent, integrated personality. As we saw in chapter 1, they don't seem to have developed the cohesive sense of *self* that could give them inner stability and security.

Everyone's personality has inner parts that are almost like little autonomous subpersonalities within the overall personality (Schwartz 1995). We acknowledge our inner multiplicity (Goulding and Schwartz 2002) when we say things like, "I don't know what got into me," "You don't seem like yourself today," or "Part of me wants to, but then another part doesn't." Various therapists have called these personality aspects the *inner child* (Bradshaw 1990; Whitfield 1987; Capacchione 1991), internal *roles* and *voices* (Berne 1964; Stone and Stone 1989), or the *internal family system* (Schwartz 1995). Having different aspects to your personality is not a clinical condition, such as "multiple personality" disorder, but is a natural characteristic of human personality.

For emotionally healthy people, their personality parts function together in a conscious, well-integrated way, like a smoothly functioning committee. However, the EI parent's personality parts remain isolated and contradictory. Lacking good personality integration, defensive EI personality parts can suddenly take over without warning. The unexpected activation of these contradictory personality parts explains the often-astonishing inconsistencies of EI parents.

EIPs and EI parents keep themselves emotionally safe by interacting through their wariest and most protective personality parts (Schwartz 1995). Occasionally they will let their guard down—such as when they fall in love—but turmoil and mistrust may soon return because their protective parts won't allow true emotional intimacy for long. When closeness looms, these protective parts soon find a reason to get suspicious, accuse others, or start fights. This is why EIPs can share tender moments at times, yet be unable to tolerate sustained closeness.

You Might Fear You're Emotionally Immature Too

As you read about parental emotional immaturity, you might wonder whether you've been an EI parent to your child at times. That would be understandable because all of us have felt uninterested, overly busy, envious, agitated, or inconsistent at times. The difference is that for emotionally connected people, these are passing states that don't interfere with their relationship capacity.

If you are reading this book, you are probably acutely aware of how you may have suffered from a lack of connection with your parents. You probably know what it's like to not feel important or to have low self-worth due to emotional deprivation or abuse. This self-awareness probably means you'll think about your effect on your children, and you likely won't pass down the same kind of emotional pain in your parenting.

The fact that you would even worry about affecting your children puts you at low risk for emotional immaturity. Concern about being emotionally immature suggests you can self-reflect, feel empathy for others, and have a desire for psychological self-improvement, qualities rarely found in EIPs. We all make mistakes or hurt others at times, but if you are interested in what goes on inside other people and sense their feelings, if you are careful to nurture your relationships and take responsibility for your role in a problem, you are by definition adequately emotionally mature.

Having EI parents doesn't mean you will be an emotionally immature parent yourself. In fact, you might be the one in your family tree to finally stop the multigenerational transfer of emotional pain. All you have to do is notice how your child is feeling, listen to them with empathy, and let them know that they are securely held in your heart. Apologize when you're wrong, take them completely seriously, forego sarcasm and mockery, and treat them with respect. When a child knows you are present, respectful, empathetic, and fair, they won't feel the emotional loneliness you may have felt.

Why You Keep Hoping and Trying for a Relationship

Given how hurtful and lonely relationships with EI parents can be, why would their adult child keep trying to connect with them? Why do adult children still hope that they can get their parents to be sensitive and respectful, even when those parents are frequently hurtful or domineering? The answer is that they give you occasional reasons to keep hoping, and it can take a long time to adjust expectations. Let's look at why an adult child of EI parents might keep trying.

Sometimes EI Parents Do Meet Your Needs

Children will stop hoping for connection only if a parent is *consistently* disengaged and rejecting. Such parents are closed doors, and their children know it. But parents who are *sometimes* emotionally available will keep you hoping for more. Once in a while, on good days, they drop their guard and connect enough for you to enjoy them. These fleeting pleasant experiences keep hope alive in children of all ages that one day they will have a nourishing bond with their parent.

For example, you may have shared special times with your parent and enjoyed affectionate and lighthearted moments. In such unguarded moments, your EI parent might have been less rigid and shown a tenderness or camaraderie that made it all worth it. When they were feeling good, they might have been playful, taken you along for the ride, and drawn you into their fun. During these good times, your parent might have enjoyed getting to be a child again with you. As long as you were excited about doing what the EI parent enjoyed, all was good.

But when an EI parent has to think about their child's feelings or make an effort for the child's benefit, the fun may stop. They make it clear that you should want what they want if good times are to continue. They may guide you into compliance by saying things like, "Isn't this fun?" or "You don't want to do that, do you?" coaxing the answer they want. EI parents cool off fast when the child's desires conflict with their own.

EI parents can also be very generous at times, but with a catch. They often think of their own tastes first and give the child what they themselves would like to get. Their gifts often reflect the parent's interests, not the child's preferences. It's as though they were subconsciously giving to themselves by proxy. Other times, EI parents pick out generic childhood gifts without considering their child's unique interests. But of course, sometimes they do get it exactly right, and your hopes about being known and loved spring up again.

Other times EI parents lower their defenses and open up when under duress, such as in extreme adversity or even while dying. Under these extraordinary conditions, some EI parents reflect on their behavior and express remorse. These glimpses of deeper relatedness can feel precious, but if the child were to try to go further, the parent might shut down again. Unfortunately, the EI parent's defensiveness makes it impossible for them to sustain that deeper openness.

You Feel a Bond and Think a Relationship Is Possible

Bonding and *relationship* are two separate things (Stern 2004). Bonding is a sense of secure belonging created through familiarity and physical proximity (Bowlby 1979). Bonding gives a sense of family and tribal community, but a relationship satisfies the emotional urge to know and be known by another person. You can feel very bonded to a person, even if they show little relational interest in your subjective experience (Stern 2004).

Adult children of EI parents can feel bonded to their parents and assume it is the same thing as being loved, which it isn't. Yet when the bond feels strong, it feels like a satisfying relationship *should* be possible. Unfortunately, this doesn't necessarily follow. To distinguish between bonding and relationship, ask yourself whether the person to whom you feel bonded is aware of your inner emotional states and subjective experience. Without that interested, empathetic component, your relationship may be based more on bonding than relational love.

As part of your recovery from emotional takeovers by EI parents, you may have to reeducate yourself that bonding is not the same thing as a close relationship. As an adult, you might be better off investing in a deeper relationship with yourself, while lowering your expectations for the kind of relationship you can have with an emotionally unresponsive parent.

You Project Your Maturity and Strengths onto Them

Most of us know about projection as a negative psychological defense, such as projecting our faults onto others or fearing unrealistically that someone's out to get us. But erroneously projecting our own *positive* qualities onto other people is almost as big a problem. Adult children of EI parents are especially likely to assume others are psychologically similar, seeing too much maturity or potential in people. It's okay to give someone the benefit of the doubt, but not to the point where you expect them to show behaviors they are incapable of. This overoptimism is a habit formed early in life when a child needed to believe in a parent's goodness.

Whether it's with an EI parent or another adult relationship, it's crucial to be discerning about the differences between EI personality characteristics and your own qualities. You don't want to get these mixed up by projecting your strengths and sensitivities onto them. You want to see them as they are so you can make informed choices about the kind of relationship that's possible.

Reality May Be Too Painful to See

EI parents can be so disappointing in their emotional unavailability that children can't bear to see them as they are. Children often protect their developing psyches by holding on to illusions of connection with their EI parent. They magnify their parent's good qualities so it seems they do have a connection, even if that parent might be emotionally destructive or distant toward them. I've seen this with psychotherapy clients who initially describe their childhood and parents in glowing terms, only to realize later how little they received emotionally.

Fantasies about a good, close relationship are often preferable to facing how little empathy you got and how illusory your connection may have been. Some of the most productive moments for people in psychotherapy are when they face the emotional truth of what they never received. They may become sad and angry, but then they become more interested in seeking connection with other people. You can begin this process in the next exercise, but please consider psychotherapy or support groups to help you with any strong feelings that might come up.

Exercise: What You May Have Lost

To start this process, get your journal and take some quiet time to reflect on what you may have lost in childhood as a result of having EI parents. (Looking at a childhood photograph of yourself as you do this exercise can make it especially meaningful.) Next, complete these sentences and follow up with thoughts on what you wrote.

I lost the chance to be…

I didn't have the opportunity to feel…

It hurt, but I learned to accept…

I wish I'd never been made to feel.…

If I had had a magic wand, I would've made my mother more…

If I had had a magic wand, I would've made my father more…

I just wanted someone to…

After completing your reflections on what you wrote, let your inner child self know that you will now give yourself the attention and acceptance you may have lost and will look for more interested, reciprocal people to be close to.

Why Can't They Change?

Adult children of EI parents are prone to *healing fantasies* (Gibson 2015) in which they secretly hope that they can change their parents and have a rewarding relationship with them. Remember Gina from chapter 2, whose elderly parents wanted to move near her? Gina confessed that one of the reasons she even considered their demand was the fantasy that one day her critical, explosive father might open up to her, finally giving them an opportunity to connect. She worried that she might be shutting the door on that last chance for closeness if she didn't let them do what they wanted.

These healing fantasies should be questioned because they prolong an improbable hope for parental change. Instead, you are more likely to be healed by your own efforts than anything your parents might do. Whatever does improve in your relationship with EI parents will likely be caused by a shift in your outlook, not a change in them.

It's understandable that if you crave your parents' interest and connection, you might think they'd want the same thing. But any attempts by you to change your EI parents are unlikely to work because they are easily destabilized by the emotional intensity of such encounters. When you attempt emotional closeness with an EI parent, their instinct is to pull back. You think you're trying to give love, but it may feel uncomfortable to them. They have already formed a personality style that protects them. They don't want to change.

Having suppressed so many of their own deeper needs for connection, EI parents just don't get what all the fuss is about. They may not understand why this is so important to you because they don't realize how crucial their relationship is for their child's emotional security and self-esteem. Many EI parents have such low self-worth that they can't imagine that their presence and interest would matter so much to their children. It is nearly impossible for these parents to believe how much they have to offer just by being there for their children.

Sadness About Giving Up Your Healing Fantasy

Accepting your EI parent's limitations can help you have more realistic expectations, but it can be hard to give up the dream that they could change and become the loving parent you needed. That fantasy has probably helped you through tough times with them, hoping that one day they would make up for the emotional loneliness and self-doubts they caused. But instead of wishful thinking, perhaps it would work better to come to grips with what is.

The Need to Grieve

Releasing hopeful fantasies feels like a real loss. You can't give up something so important without allowing room for grief.

As you grieve the loss of illusions about your parents, you may also feel sad for what you had to sacrifice in yourself in order to adapt to your EI parent. Allowing sadness about your own self-repression will put you back in touch with lost parts of yourself that didn't get to be heard before. I hope you will listen to them now because working through the grief of these suppressed parts will make you free to be your whole self and feel complete.

When you stop hoping that your EI parent might one day change, you can finally face how hurt, alone, and frightened you felt as a child. Awareness of the cost of these emotional injuries probably had to be suppressed in childhood so you could complete the business of growing up. It was healthy for you back then to hope that your EI parent might one day care about your feelings and seek a deeper connection. But now as an adult, it is healthier to give up hopes for your parent's change. When you stop longing to be rescued by them, you can connect with your own emotional needs and thereby bond more securely to yourself, your future development, and your future relationships.

Choose Your Active Self over Your Suffering Self

As a child with EI parents, some part of yourself may have figured out that the best way to get along was to suffer in silence and not rock the boat. This *suffering self* (Forbes 2018; Perkins 1995) adapts to a dominating parent by staying powerless in life and passive in relationships. Rather than feeling anger or knowing what it wants, the suffering self stays stuck in chronic unhappiness and feelings of helplessness. It had to relinquish assertiveness as it tried to adjust to a difficult childhood situation, but it shouldn't be allowed to keep running the show (Schwartz 1995).

The suffering self convinces you that self-sacrifice makes you a good person or at least more likely to be loved by others. But now this suffering self should be retired as the model for your relationships. Being active on your own behalf is much better than passivity and helplessness as a way of dealing with overbearing parents. As an adult, you can now take action toward what is best for your optimal energy and self-care.

Adjust Your Expectations and Work on Yourself

Now that you have read about healing fantasies, ask yourself whether it's possible that what you crave is not really a closer *relationship* with these particular parents but more the *feeling* that you are lovable and acceptable. Would you pick your parent as a desirable new friend you'd be happy to have? If not, maybe you can feel good about yourself in another way. Maybe you don't need your parent to love you in order to feel lovable. Is it possible that as an adult, you could give it to yourself through a more caring relationship with yourself?

The second half of this book will focus on how to have a fulfilling relationship with yourself by exploring your inner world, setting fresh intentions, and updating your self-concept. You'll learn to support your own self-growth, open your heart to better relationships and more fun, while strengthening your unique sense of identity and individuality.

Through these practices, your self-development will be pursued for its own sake, not as a secret way to finally win an EI parent's approval.

In the meantime, you can trade in your longing for a more satisfying relationship with your EI parent for new goals of seeing them more realistically, understanding their limitations, and adjusting your expectations. As long as you hold on to hopes they can't fulfill, the relationship will be frustrating for both of you.

You can't change them, and you can't make them happy. Even if you knock yourself out, the best you will do is briefly lessen their discontent. That's because even though their emotionally immature relationship system (EIRS) makes it feel like you are responsible for their happiness, their emotional limits don't allow them to absorb what you try to give them.

Your heart will feel lighter once you accept that you can't make them happy, fix their lives, or make them proud of you. It's usually beyond them to think about your feelings, and they can't sustain reciprocal emotional intimacies. They won't listen to you for long, and nothing you do may ever be enough. They'll continue to see you in the role as their child, not a full capable adult. They'll exert dominance and demand to be the most important person in the relationship. Their interests will always come first, and even if you are a model adult, they may still be critical, demeaning, or dismissive toward you.

Raise Your Expectations for Other Relationships

If you learned in childhood that other people were more important than you, you might carry that over to adult relationships. You may believe that wanting reciprocity is expecting too much and that chronic emotional frustration is normal for relationships. Many adult children of EI parents accept statements like "Relationships take a lot of work" because that was their experience growing up. It doesn't seem odd to them to have problems requiring couples counseling before they even get married. They subconsciously *expect* dissatisfaction and poor communication in close relationships.

It can be an alien concept that a mate is supposed to be concerned for your feelings, interested in your subjective experience, and want to get along as much as you do. If you had EI parents, it can feel acceptable to settle for meager attention on another's timetable and only under certain circumstances. But once you realize that someone is occasionally giving you emotional snacks and never a satisfying connection, it frees you up to look for new sources of emotional nurturing.

If you did not get much emotionally from EI parents in childhood, you might be too willing to put a lot of one-sided effort into your adult relationships. You may not be happy, but you may feel you should take whatever's offered. Your job now is to question any one-sided relationship and look for something more satisfying. As you work at lowering your expectations for the EIPs and EI parents in your life, you should simultaneously raise your expectations in order to find friends and partners who put as much effort into reciprocal, empathetic relationships as you do.

Exercise: What You're Looking for Now

In the spirit of looking for emotional satisfactions now that you lacked in childhood, take some time to think and use your journal to fill out these statements about your new possibilities.

I now have the chance to be…

At last, I have the opportunity to feel…

Some of the behaviors I will no longer accept from people are….

I'm going to find people who are…

I'm looking for people who will…

Now I see myself as…

In summary, you don't have to be reparented by your actual parent to become what you want to be now. Once you start relying on your adult mind and listening to your own heart, you've got all you need inside you for the guidance and support you wish you'd had years ago. By valuing yourself and exploring your inner world, you will no longer feel so hurt by parents who can't see you for who you are. You don't need them to feel lovable and worthy because you can now get that from yourself and from like-minded people.

Highlights to Remember

EI parents leave their children with unmet needs for connection, communication, and approval. Instead of giving their children adequate attention and affection, many EI parents show disinterest, envy, excessive busyness, or emotional agitation. You may wish for a better relationship with them, but their defenses and inconsistencies render them unavailable at an emotional level. However, by finally accepting their limitations, you can turn your attention toward better relationships with yourself and others. Once you release and mourn what you can't get from them, you will have more realistic relationships with them, other people, and yourself as well.

Chapter 4

How to Resist Emotional Takeovers

Recognize Others' Distortions and Don't Disconnect from Yourself

Emotional takeovers occur when EIPs induce emotions and ideas in you that will help control you for their benefit. In this chapter, you'll learn to recognize emotional coercions and emotional takeovers as soon as they start. Your job is to become so aware of EIPs' psychological moves that you'll no longer get caught up in their exploitative relationship system. You'll see how EIPs achieve emotional takeovers by making their needs seem compelling, and you'll learn how to handle this without dissociating from yourself. (As I refer to EIPs in general in this chapter, keep in mind that this definitely includes all EI parents.)

Keep an Active Mindset

This chapter will show you how to actively deflect emotional takeovers and refuse to be emotionally coerced into doing what EIPs want. Instead of giving in to them, you can now remind yourself, *I can do something about what they just did.* Affirming this active mindset empowers you to stop being swept along in the slipstream of their agendas.

One woman described this active attitude as her determination not to be pressured by other people's demands. In her words, "I'm not going to be dictated by their urgency. I'm not going to allow them to come into my space and tell me how I have to be."

When you resolve to make your own decisions instead of giving in to EIPs pressure, you become less vulnerable to the subconscious pull of their emotionally immature relationship system (EIRS) and the emotional take-over it spawns. Having an *active* mindset prepares you to think for yourself instead of automatically acquiescing. By questioning their assumptions, you'll actively protect your boundaries and independence. You no longer agree that it's up to you to repair their self-esteem or stabilize their emotions.

By becoming sensitive to how EIRS pressure feels, EIPs' emotional takeovers become more obvious to you and easier to counter. Once you see what they're doing, their coercive behaviors lose their force. Instead of being their victim, you'll get back on your own side.

First, let's look at how EIPs make it seem that their issues are more important than anything that could possibly be going on with you.

You Can Challenge Their Distorted Assumptions

EIPs see the world through a kind of *distortion field* (Wald 2018) that exaggerates everything and makes their needs seem inherently more important than those of others. If you are not careful, you will accept their distortions as reality and agree that these are extraordinary circumstances and they really do deserve to come first.

Stop Accepting That They're the Most Important One

If you grew up as the child of an EI parent, it probably seemed to you that some people really were more important than anyone else. For instance, in many homes, all eyes go to the EIP as soon as they walk in the door. They are the center of attention, and everyone instinctively watches them because no one can concentrate on anything else if the EIP is in a mood. The family mythology is that this EIP is extra special and family members try hard not to upset them.

So who could blame you for thinking it's normal for one person's emotional state to rule everyone else's life? To a child who is still learning what this world is all about, the EIP's outsize status would appear to be an observable fact.

Although this kind of family domination by an EIP is not normal or healthy, there is no way for a child to know this because kids rarely see how other families operate. Children can only witness how an EIP is treated in their family and think things to themselves like, *This seems real; Dad really is the most important person in the world; Mom's feelings clearly are more important than anyone else's;* or *Of course my little sister's demands are everybody's crisis.*

But now as an adult, you know better. You have the right to think of your own needs. EI expectations to the contrary, your purpose in life is not to make someone feel more powerful than they really are. A person can't claim to be more important than anyone else just because they feel that way. You and that EIP are existential equals; no one is more important than anyone else. You're neither their possession nor their servant.

Question Whether It Is an Emergency

The EIP's distortion field turns everything into a big deal. For them, ordinary life's vicissitudes can constitute a crisis that needs to be solved *right now*. When they're upset, you should jump first and ask questions later. If you grew up with an EIP, you probably lived in stressful apprehension, poised to react as you monitored the EIP's crisis of the moment. Do you need to get out of their way? Inquire about their unhappy body language? Make sure no one disturbs them? Listen to their complaints? Calm them down? Make them feel cherished? Whatever it takes, you do it because you dread the fallout of their emotional destabilization.

It's often hard to tell whether an EIP's issues are reality-based or are just their old trauma scripts. Are they really being victimized? Did someone really attack them for no reason, or did they start it? It's hard to know. Their distortion field will tell you that nothing is their fault and everyone else is out to get them. Thankfully, you now know enough about emotional takeovers to take any EIP's urgency with a grain of salt.

From inside their distortion field, they act like you are the only solution to their pressing problems. But once their distorted self-importance no longer mesmerizes you, you will realize that, in the big scheme of things, they don't have the right to take you over, nor do they matter more than you. There are *two* human lives to be considered, not just one. It's not true that their needs make them more important or entitled than other human beings.

Don't Fall for Their Flattery

EIPs often use flattery to coax you into going along with whatever they want. They may act like you have all the answers or are uniquely strong and capable of fixing their problems. They tell you they don't know what they would do without you. (My guess is that they would soon find someone else more willing.)

EIPs offer a spectacular relationship deal: if you do what they want, then you will be *everything* to them. However, the fine print says that you are only as good as the last thing you did for them. In this distorted arrangement, you can be everything one minute and nothing the next. This is because they have an extremely self-preoccupied way of looking at relationships. You are either wonderful or useless to them—with nothing in between.

EIPs' flatteries can be very seductive to anyone. We all want to feel special. Who isn't intrigued by someone who acts like you are the answer to their prayer? It's easy to forgive them anything as soon as you feel like *everything* to them again, even if they ignore or disrespect you the rest of the time. You might put up with a lot as long as the EIP sometimes makes you feel important, lovable, and special. This use of flattery is well known in con artists, cult leaders, dictators, and other exploiters to help get their foot in the door. They know people need to feel special, and they use it to cement their power.

You don't have to let any of these flatteries work on you. None of these enticements offer a relationship deal that makes sense on any level.

Besides, do you really *want* to be their special person they can call on any time? Wouldn't you prefer genuine people who show you kindness and sincere interest, not just puffery they bestow because they're in a good mood and about to get what they want?

Getting Free of Their Distortion Field

Now let's see how to step back and ask the right questions that can free you from the EIP's distortion field of being more important than you are.

Assess Their Urgency

EIPs exaggerate everything. Like small children, every frustration or insult is the end of the world. They are like the boy who cried wolf; you don't know whether to believe them or not. That is why it's so important not to blindly accept their completely self-focused view of their situation. It's up to *you* to clarify the reality of things. Otherwise, you will be swept up in one drama after another, all seemingly urgent and desperate. For self-protection, it pays to assess the reality of the situation and put their distorted views into perspective.

The first step in doing this is to resist the desperate urgency that usually accompanies an EIP's pleas. You don't have to exaggerate and distort along with them, and you certainly don't have to accept their twist on the facts. You are free to back up and look at their situation objectively or run it by a third party. Be sure to pin down the EIP for specifics: it's possible things aren't as urgent as they seem. Given their emotional distortions, should you be taking their word for the true magnitude of their problem?

Get Some Distance and Analyze the Problem

Don't forget that in any crisis, there is much that EIPs haven't considered because of their many distortions and fears. When faced with a serious problem, they panic. In their mind, the only answer is that someone must save them. They want you to jump in and join them in their black hole of desperation, followed by miraculously making it all better.

It's up to you to decide what level of response from you makes sense, independent of the EIP's pressure and wildfire emotions. What's the level of actual need, if any? You have to be the one who examines this because they won't. The proper response to any of their emergencies is not to jump in, but to step back and assess realities first.

Some EIPs will get huffy if you want to analyze things instead of immediately acquiescing. They are especially likely to feel betrayed if you suggest that their reactions might be causing some of their problems. They make it an issue of lack of love if you don't agree straightaway to give them what they want. But you still can tell them you're not sure their impulsive solution is the best answer, and because they're asking for your help, you want to take time to think out other possible solutions with them.

If they refuse this, they are promoting the greatest distortion of all: that you don't matter as much as they do. Fortunately, you don't have to accept this offer of a skewed, one-sided relationship. You are under no obligation to put another adult's needs ahead of your own. Explain that you don't proceed with anything without thinking about it, and let them know you'd be happy to talk later if they'd be willing to take your needs into consideration too.

Questions to Ask Yourself When in the Midst of an Emotional Takeover Attempt

What is the reality (not just what they're telling you)?

What are verifiable facts of the situation?

What's the seriousness of the crisis? Is it an emergency? For whom?

Is their request the best solution to the problem?

Could they solve it themselves once they calm down?

Should this be your responsibility?

By asking yourself these questions, you can assess whether it is a true crisis or an emotional takeover dressed up to look like one.

Identify Whether You Really Have an Obligation

When EIPs have a crisis, they make you feel obligated to help. This is the first stage of their emotional takeover: their problem is your problem. If you hesitate and want to think things through, they essentially react with, "I can't believe you're not doing this for me in my time of need!" But your job, in the face of this implied accusation, is to step back and ask yourself whether you really *do* have an obligation, under *these* circumstances, with *these* events in play. Otherwise, you will be yielding to a full emotional takeover by giving them the right to be the voice of your conscience.

No one but you has the right to define your obligation and duty in a relationship. The EIP's urgency implies that you have no choice. But of course you do. You are not a bad person for wanting to think it over or to look for ways to help without sacrificing your own well-being. Remember to ask yourself: *Is it an emergency? Is this the best solution? Is this my responsibility?* You have the right to examine for yourself all the things they think you should do. Clarify everyone's responsibilities by considering: *What's me, what's them, and what—if anything—is really an obligation?*

When you start feeling compelled by duty or obligation, ask yourself who's suggesting that and why. There can't be only one acceptable option—not when two or more people are involved. By working together, you two could figure out something that works for *both* of you. Ask yourself, as Byron Katie (2002) suggests, Is this "obligation" you feel an absolute, cosmic *truth*? Rational inquiry will reveal that one EIP's opinion isn't the only way to look at things.

Step Back from Enabling Them

Enabling is when you rescue people from the repeated consequences of their own actions or do things for them that they could do on their own. Enabling weakens the resourcefulness of the other person because you continue to make yourself the answer to their problems. You are agreeing with them that their problem is impossible for them to deal with by themselves. Enabling offers the EIP the right to take over your life.

When EIPs are caught up in their distortion fields, they panic and may not be able to see alternatives. This isn't because the alternatives aren't there; it's because they don't give themselves enough time to see them. Because EIPs rush through everything, you'll feel pressured to jump in immediately. But when you intervene too quickly, it confirms their belief that someone else needs to figure it out for them. This reinforces their alarmed and demanding reactivity.

————Bert's Story————

Bert got a panicky phone call from his younger brother, Tom, asking for a $10,000 loan for what Bert thought was an impulsive solution to a larger debt problem. He encouraged Tom to give it some more thought. As a delay tactic to slow down the situation, Bert also asked Tom to write down the details of the whole situation for him. This would give Bert some space to think about what he was willing to do, plus it would give Tom some practice in sitting down and working through a problem by writing. But Tom was offended: he didn't see what good that would do and just wanted the money. Tom's irritation revealed his underlying assumption of entitlement: Tom expected Bert to give him $10,000 and yet was affronted by a reasonable request to specify in writing the nature of his problem. No lending institution would contemplate a loan without the same request.

It's amazing, given their urgency, but sometimes if you don't get back to EIPs right away, the problem resolves itself. It's not unusual that you might still be worrying about an EIP's crisis, only to find out later the EIP had already moved on, gone to sleep, or found something else to make them feel better. It's good to remember that, by definition, any emergency seen from inside a distortion field might be distorted.

Just remember, you have the right to take your time and consider whether you really want to help or not. You don't have to let yourself be coerced into helping against your better judgment.

Decide Beforehand What You Are Willing to Give

Think in advance about what you are willing to commit to: under what circumstances would you intervene, and when would you not? This should be a detailed, thoughtful exercise, made far in advance of the next call on your assistance. Have some idea of your acceptable limits *before* you enter their distortion zone.

For instance, you might be okay with paying their rent one month, but only if you give the money directly to the landlord. Or you might be willing to assist, but only after they've done some things to help themselves. Those decisions should come from you, and you have every right to ask questions about their situation and not accept their assessment at face value. You might be able to suggest other forms of help they can't see from inside their distortion field.

In another example, an older couple had spent thousands of dollars trying to get their addicted son straight and employed. He had stolen from them yet kept asking for one more loan. The couple finally stepped back and assessed how much they were willing to give in the future and under what conditions. They thought about all kinds of dire scenarios that could arise and drew lines over how far they'd go. Then they were ready when their son later suggested that maybe he could just move in with them. They already knew that his lifestyle would not fit their retirement situation. Their health and marriage took precedence. They weren't vulnerable to his emotional takeover or coercion because they had thought things out in advance.

Exercise: Prepare for the Next Time

Think of EIPs in your life who often expect you to go along with them or give them help. Prepare yourself for the next time by making a list of everything you would or wouldn't be willing to do. It should range from things you wouldn't hesitate to grant (they are thirsty and you give them water), to things that give you pause (they want you to go on a family vacation), all the way down to requests you could refuse with no guilt (they want you to buy them something expensive because their friends have one). On the continuum of these possibilities, imagine and rank hypothetical future situations where you would or wouldn't want to help. You may never face these exact situations, but this exercise will give you practice in thinking about your comfortable limits beforehand.

Important Exceptions to Refusing a Request

We're not always as strong as we want to be, so sometimes you might go ahead and give in because you are too worn down or bewildered to do otherwise. That's okay. Just notice how it feels to be taken over and make a note for the future. Other times, situations feel too serious to just say no, and you might end up helping because the risks of not acting seem too high.

You Might Decide to Help When a Life Is at Risk

A life at risk is a good exception to make when agreeing to help. For instance, one man decided to pay for a cheap motel room for his irascible, homeless, and addicted brother during the winter because his brother had been admitted to the hospital with hypothermia. His brother was impossible to deal with, but he didn't want the man to freeze to death either.

Another challenging situation might be when people talk about committing suicide. Is it distortion, panic, or the real thing? When the stakes are that high, you should act to save their life by calling the police or other professionals to intervene. They will then know that if they ever call you again in such a situation, you'll protect them by calling the police to keep them safe. Suicide threats are the most chilling form of emotional takeover. You cannot allow yourself to get cast in the role of the only person who can save their life through your efforts alone. Suicide threats should be treated like hostage situations where someone could really get hurt.

You wouldn't try to deal with it yourself; you would call in law enforcement specialists.

You Might Have an Innocent Third Party to Consider

Sometimes you may *choose* to go along with an EIP's demands because of an innocent third party. After looking at the situation carefully, you might discover you want the same thing they want, but perhaps for different reasons. For instance, Stan's adult daughter Layla had begged money from him numerous times and spent it irresponsibly. However, Stan agreed to help her buy a newer car with airbags for the safety of his ten-year-old grandson.

Why You Become Vulnerable to Emotional Takeovers

We can be reluctant to set limits because EIPs stir up emotions that get us to do what they want. You might give in to an emotional takeover because

- you feel bad about yourself for saying no

- you are afraid of their anger

- you fear being judged and punished.

Let's look at each one of these fears, and what to do about it in order to preserve your emotional autonomy when EIPs put on the pressure.

1. You Feel Bad About Yourself for Saying No

If normal standing up for yourself feels selfish, your self-esteem is probably being held hostage by an EIP. With EIPs, you can't say no to a request and still be seen as caring. Only in the distorted world of the EIP could thinking things over or setting a limit be construed as mean or uncaring. But their hurt reaction can be quite effective because no one wants to be a villain, and no decent person likes to be seen as uncaring.

However, you can correct their distortions by saying something non-threatening like, "I'm not intending to be mean. Do you think it's unloving to have a different viewpoint from yours?" Or you could say, "You and I see this differently, and that's because we each have responsibility for our own lives."

2. You're Afraid of Their Anger

You may also allow emotional takeovers because you fear the EIP's temper. They make us nervous with their emotional reactivity, much like people tiptoe around a sleeping baby or hesitate to say no to a volcanic toddler. Very controlling or narcissistic EIPs can get enraged if you don't conform to their wishes. The EIP may not act it out in physically harmful ways (or they might), but you will feel the anger radiating off them like a furnace. You feel like they might explode any minute.

With volatile EIPs, it's always a good idea to set limits with them under safe circumstances, such as speaking on the phone instead of in person or talking in places where other people are nearby for support or protection. When you talk to them, set your limits without being critical, judgmental, or getting in their face. You can try saying something like, "I know, I wish I could give you what you want, but I'm not going to be able to do that this time," or "Yeah, I don't blame you for being mad. It's just more than I can do right now."

Of course, if there is any question of potential physical violence, you must consult with experts to figure out how to handle the situation safely.

3. You Fear Being Judged and Punished

When you incur an EIP's judgment, it's sometimes hard to figure out exactly what was so bad about what you did. They act appalled, but you don't see how what you did was so horrible. Remember that EIPs think in emotional absolutes, which means that if you aren't completely on their side, they may see you as the enemy.

Many adult children of EI parents suffer from intense, irrational fears about being judged and punished. These fears of punitive judgment can come from EI parents, older siblings, teachers, or any authority figure.

When this childhood fear resurfaces, it feels terrifying, as if there were no hope and your downfall were imminent. When these fears of punishment get triggered, you start thinking things like, *This will be the end of me. It's never going to get better. I'm totally screwed.*

For instance, my client Betsy sometimes woke up in the middle of the night with a pounding heart, feeling like something dreadful was about to happen to her. She lived in constant fear that someone in authority, perhaps a boss, was watching her like a hawk and waiting for her to fail. In her childhood, her moralistic parents had been so scrupulously judgmental and punitive that she never felt safe at home. They frequently punished her for things she didn't even know she had done wrong. Betsy remembered as a little girl she only felt truly safe when she could hear her mother vacuuming or talking on the phone because then she knew she wasn't about to be punished.

The good thing about judgment is that you have to agree with it in order to feel bad. They may judge you, but you alone determine whether you feel guilty or not. You can step out of any EIP's distorted judgments as soon as you feel free to disagree with their opinions. You can decline to accept their criticism and make a distinction between what they're saying about you and what you know to be true about yourself. Remember, just because an EIP *feels* something is true, doesn't necessarily mean it *is*. You get to define yourself, not them. Decline their judgment if you don't think it's fair.

All of us can sometimes fall into EI takeovers that make us feel so bad that we emotionally disconnect from ourselves in order to stop the hurt or fear. Unfortunately, this self-protective disconnection just makes it easier for the EIP's negative distortions to take over our minds and hearts.

The Dissociation Reaction: Why You Can't Think of a Thing to Say

Let's shift gears now and look at how a loss of connection with your own feelings facilitates emotional takeovers by EIPs. *Dissociation* is when you psychologically separate from yourself. It can make you freeze up or shrivel inside, or even make you feel like you're detached from your body.

Most people have heard about dissociation only from dramatic stories about people with "multiple personalities." But dissociation is a natural defense and can be any form of distancing from your conscious experience of yourself. It's a primitive type of emotional escape and a very common psychological defense against threat or danger, especially for children in an unsafe environment. Think of it as an automatic shutdown valve; it doesn't fix what's wrong, but it stops you from being emotionally overwhelmed by it.

Dissociating—or separating—from your self-connection makes you passive and lets you get sucked into an EIP's emotional takeover. Unfortunately, this self-disconnection can become so automatic that you might not know when you are sliding into it.

The Disconnection State and Its Roots

Slipping into a dissociated, disconnected state is one of the ways we instinctively cope with imminent danger. It's related to the play-dead or freeze response in animals that occurs when they realize a predator is too close for escape. You might have personally experienced dissociation as a stunned feeling, a kind of trance-like state accompanied by a feeling of blankness and loss of initiative. You can't think what to say or do. Everyone is familiar with this shutdown state: we call it the deer-in-the-headlights reaction.

Under the most extreme stress, dissociative disconnection sometimes can make people feel like they've exited their bodies, as if they are outside themselves or hovering above, watching what's happening to them. This is a common trauma response and shows how easily anyone can disconnect to the point where they remain aware but can no longer act.

Dissociation saves us from overwhelming levels of traumatic pain, injury, and loss. Sometimes it is a blessing to step away from yourself and feel nothing. For instance, some forms of self-disconnection can help an injured person keep fighting to survive without the distraction of pain. Likewise, a bereft person can face inconceivable loss by going into a numb, shutdown mode. People who overuse intoxicants induce dissociated states in an artificial way, setting aside their ordinary consciousness to not be aware of their feelings.

This same dissociative mechanism can cause you to go blank and let an EIP emotionally control you. When you can't think of what to say in response to a hurtful remark or unreasonable demand, dissociation may be happening on a small scale. You're in a little state of shock and can't think.

We can learn dissociative practices early in life by being around emotionally reactive EI parents. You may have needed to disconnect from your feelings in order to cope with parents who had a short temper or emotionally abandoned you. Once children discover how self-disconnection takes away pain, they can use it for increasingly minor threats. After a while, they can become strangers to their own inner experience; instead of just cutting themselves off from fear or hurt, all emotion gets so dulled that life itself feels a little unreal.

Why It's So Important Not to Disconnect from Yourself

Once you shift into self-disconnection, you can no longer make choices in a situation. Therefore, learning to recognize and prevent dissociation is crucial. The steps in preventing dissociation are to

1. stay in touch with yourself no matter what

2. snap out of it when you start to zone out

3. keep thinking of active ways to deal with the situation.

When escape from EIPs is hard, such as during family events, it can be tempting to unhook from your self-awareness and just float along until you can get away from them. But disconnecting from yourself affirms that you are powerless when it comes to them—which is just not true. It also makes you feel more helpless and ineffective in the long run.

——Brendan's Story——

Brendan dreaded his widowed mother's yearly visits. He told me he had learned to "put himself away" as soon as she arrived. Growing up, this passive solution felt like the only way to preserve his individuality around his critical, intrusive, and controlling mother. It felt better to disconnect from his real self than to be picked apart by her criticisms. As a child, expressing his feelings to her had only resulted in mockery, rejection, or getting him thrown out of the house.

However, Brendan's withdrawal and detachment came at a price: he felt like he entered a state of suspended animation while his mother was visiting, followed by intense cravings for junk food and alcohol as soon as she left. Brendan's self-defeating solution was to make himself "empty" so he would be less of an emotional target for her and then use bingeing to refuel after her visits. Eating and drinking were experiences under his control and, unlike his mother, guaranteed to give him something back.

Brendan's first step in changing things with his mother was to stop dissociating from himself and allowing her to be the center of attention. I encouraged him to stay connected with his true thoughts and feelings and be active rather than passive when it came to handling her self-centered behavior. Brendan started interrupting her one-sided "conversations," rather than listening to her to the point of numbness. When he felt himself start to drift, he abruptly changed the subject, stood up, walked outside, or otherwise physically interrupted their interaction. Brendan was learning to actively take breaks from her, rather than from himself.

As Brendan stopped disconnecting from himself, he became more active on his own behalf. When his mother made unwanted suggestions about his job, Brendan explained he didn't want advice and asked her just to listen sympathetically. When she planned to stay a week, he cut it down to two days. Brendan also used a different response to his mother's critical comments; instead of zoning out, he would immediately say, "Wait a minute... wait a minute...let me think about what you just said." He thus interrupted his own dissociative habit, giving himself time to realize how she was making him feel, and telling her about it. He may have curtailed his mother's own dissociative traits too, because many times EIPs' excessive verbiage is a dissociative way of keeping themselves separated from deeper feelings they don't want to be aware of.

Like Brendan, you too can intend to stay conscious and connected with yourself during interactions with an EIP or EI parent. It's worth practicing because once you stop dissociating and stay connected with yourself, you will no longer be susceptible to emotional takeovers. In chapter 7, we will look at more methods and skills for regaining your self-connection.

Highlights to Remember

In this chapter, we looked at how to spot and resist tactics used by EIPs for emotional takeovers. You learned about EIPs' distortion fields and how they use their sense of urgency as entitlement to your help. You now can claim your right to take time to think your way through situations when you feel pressured to do more than you want to. You can now recognize an EIP's exaggerations and consciously and actively refuse any request that makes you uncomfortable. You also hopefully realize how an EIP's intimidating pressure, anger, and judgments can disconnect you from yourself to the point of dissociation. You learned about the importance of taking charge and acting on your own behalf in any situation that might threaten to separate you from yourself.

Chapter 5

Skills to Manage Interactions and Evade Coercions

Actions That Empower You

Interactions with EI parents can leave you feeling inarticulate, controlled, and powerless. If you grew up with EI parents, you probably didn't learn skills for handling emotional coercion and exploitation. But now as an adult, you'll be able to respond in new ways. In this chapter, you'll learn how to establish boundaries and evade an EI parent's takeover tactics.

However, please be sure to adapt these new skills to fit *your* personality style so they're within your comfort zone. Some assertiveness skills can feel so extreme they seem to require a whole new personality. Overly blunt assertiveness can be uncomfortable to the point that even if you could do it, you wouldn't want to do it more than once or twice. For example, flat refusals and just saying no may work for some people, but it might not be your style. You may be more comfortable apologizing, demurring, and pleasing your way forward. The following skills will still work even if you're hesitant, accommodating, or sweet by nature. If you end up with the outcome you intended in an EIP interaction, that's all that counts.

Guidelines That Will Make Your Skills More Effective

First, let's first look at a few basic reminders that will make these skills more effective.

You Can Take Your Time

You may have noticed how rushed you feel around EIPs, as if you are irritating them by taking a moment to think. They are always hurrying their children and making everyone tense and uncomfortable with their low tolerance for delay. Because they are so self-preoccupied and have such low empathy, they can't see why others can't instantly give them what they want.

It's easy to succumb to their urgency. Most people get flummoxed when rushed, which then opens the door wider to the EIP's emotional takeover. Before you know it, *you* will be pressuring yourself to do everything for them quickly. Once you start hurrying yourself, EIPs easily gain control of your emotional state.

Taking your time prevents emotional takeovers because you stay in touch with yourself. One of the most self-preserving things you can say to an EIP is "I need some time to think about that." EIPs hate that phrase because, in their mind, there's no need to waste time thinking. They don't see why they can't speed things along by *telling* you what to think.

Don't agree to do things according to their time frame. You need *time* to consider what you're willing to engage in and what you aren't. If you rush yourself, you will be moving forward without benefit of your own self-awareness. Then it's a sure bet that you will end up serving the EIP's needs, not your own.

Figure Out the Exact Outcome You Want

Focus on how you want *each* interaction with an EIP to turn out. Aim your actions toward your preferred outcome, rather than worrying about what the EIP wants. If you don't have a clear outcome in mind, the EIP will take over by default with their more rigid and single-minded approach.

Setting the outcome you want gives every interaction much-needed structure and direction. Structure keeps your goals in sight so an EIP's insistence doesn't make you lose track of what's important to you.

To identify the desired outcome for an interaction, ask yourself the following questions.

- If I got what I wanted from this interaction, what would that look like? (Perhaps you set a limit with them and only agree to what you really want to do.)

- Is the outcome I'm considering within my control, or is it up to them? (Try picking a goal that *you* can make happen.)

- Am I fixated on needing them to act differently? (If you're looking for them to change, how about picking a different outcome that is within your power.)

- Is my goal for this interaction my internal growth, acting differently, or both? (You could promote your growth by staying aware of your feelings or try new behaviors by speaking up when you disagree.)

Reviewing this checklist in advance keeps you focused so you don't come out of interactions agreeing to something you didn't want. Avoid any regret by making your preferred outcome a priority in the first place.

Don't Take Immature Behavior So Seriously: Just Be Persistent

EIPs like to tell you what you should do, even when the decision is clearly yours. To evade this inappropriate pressure, here's what to do. Acknowledge their objections if you want ("Uh-huh," "I hear you," "Mmmm"), but don't take them seriously. Vaguely listen for a minute, keep a light tone, smile pleasantly, and then repeat what you want or what you are planning to do (Smith 1975). If you encounter resistance, don't make a big deal out of it: just keep restating what you said before. It's not a dramatic technique, but like a river carves rock, it works.

You don't argue because you don't accept the premise that your preference is anything to debate. You have made your decision. Arguing implies a legitimate contest of wills, and that, I hope, is not your goal. By simply repeating your decision, you remind the EIP that there are two points of view because—lest the EIP forget—you are two *different* people.

Vicki's Story

Vicki was not planning to attend Thanksgiving dinner at her parents' home as usual because she and her husband wanted to join his family that year. When her mother, Maureen, brought up Thanksgiving, Vicki said it might be difficult to arrange this year and she would get back to her as soon as she knew.

Vicki already knew what she was going to do, but she was giving Maureen a little time to get used to the idea before she actually declined. When Vicki finally told Maureen they weren't coming, Maureen predictably acted offended and rejected. Vicki started to cringe but immediately reminded herself not to take her mother's feelings so seriously. Vicki could see Maureen's distortion field ("This is terrible; I should come first in your plans.") in full operation, and she reminded herself not to take on guilt because her mother wasn't getting her way.

Vicki kept deflecting Maureen's line of fire by smiling and taking it lightly. She just kept repeating her plans: "You're right, Mom; it certainly will be different. I know you want us there, but this year just won't work out for us." This repeating-yourself technique is a simple, honest way of sticking to your guns.

The only thing Vicki had to do was to say the same thing pleasantly as many times as necessary until her mother brought it up less frequently. Notice that I didn't say until her mother dropped it. You can't expect EIPs to stop angling for what they want, but you can make it less rewarding for them to continue.

———Jamal's Story———

Jamal decided to quit his first job after only a year and go to a start-up company that looked like more fun. When his domineering father heard about it, he was furious. He warned Jamal that he was being stupid and that it would look bad on his resumé. Jamal said, "You might be right, Dad, but it's an opportunity I don't want to pass up." When his father kept arguing with him, Jamal just kept repeating, "You could be right, Dad, but I think it'll work out fine."

Both Vicki's mother and Jamal's father were asserting their "right" to judge their adult children's decisions. Fortunately, neither Vicki nor Jamal took their parent's indignant reactions seriously. They accepted their parent's right to feel the way they did, but they didn't agree to their demands. Notice how both Vicki and Jamal stayed in touch with their goals in the face of their parent's displeasure.

Vicki and Jamal wisely didn't argue with their parent's feelings because how their parents felt wasn't the issue. The only issue was their adult right to make their own choices. By deciding the outcome in advance, there was no room for their parents to coerce them with guilt, shame, or fear. Vicki didn't have to solve her mother's hurt feelings for her, and Jamal didn't have to convince his father.

Five Effective Skills for Dealing with EI Parents

To deal effectively with EI parents, there are five things you can do to make you immune to their emotional takeovers and distortions.

1. Step out of your rescuer role.

2. Be slippery and sidestep.

3. Lead the interaction.

4. Create space for yourself.

5. Stop them.

1. Step Out of Your Rescuer Role

Many adult children of EI parents feel they have to be their parent's rescuer or protector. These are the *internalizing* types I described in my previous book (Gibson 2015). Internalizers are perceptive, sensitive, and often let empathy for other people overrule their own preferences. They take everything to heart, assuming responsibility where there may be none. Internalizers try to jump in to solve an EIP's problem even before they ask for it. This over-responsibility is a form of *codependency* (Beattie 1987) whereby you try to feel lovable and valuable by taking on other people's problems as your own, often without being asked. You end up more consumed with their lives than your own.

2. Be Slippery and Sidestep

Being slippery is the art of sidestepping an EIP's attempt to pressure you into doing what they want. Sidestepping works better than blunt refusals when EIPs get stuck in coercion mode.

When EIPs are trying to get control, they pressure, nag, or argue, probing for your reaction so they have something to push against. Their subtext demand is, "Be subordinate, validate my views, and play the role that lets me win." However, instead of getting pulled into a struggle, you could pause for an empowering moment of self-awareness and simply say, "I don't know," or "I can't really answer that right now."

If EIPs try to prompt an argument, you can enjoy a nice breath, then sidestep them with, "I guess I don't have anything to say about that right now." Another slippery response to anything that seems false or crazy is to make noncommittal sounds, like "Uh-huh," "Hmmm," or just, "Huh." Slipperiness is effective because no friction is created, and your minimal feedback makes you a less desirable opponent.

Think of this skill as flowing around an obstacle instead of making yourself a target. Because EIPs aren't mature enough to fight fair, confrontations with them are full of dirty tricks and red herrings. They will wear you down and distract you from the outcome you want. If you accept a battle of wills, they might win because their self-centered arguments will exhaust your brain just trying to make sense of their illogical responses.

Try agreeing with their feelings. A masterful sidestep is to *agree with the EIP's feelings*. This method must be sincere and not manipulative, or it won't be effective. If you do it cynically or sarcastically, it will increase your emotional reactivity to them, not lower it.

First you detach from them emotionally and accept their right to feel whatever they feel, just as you hold that right for yourself. You don't have to judge their feelings, nor do you have to do what they want. You understand that EIPs are upset when things don't go their way, yet you don't change your mind just because they're unhappy.

This can be hard to do when EIPs or EI parents start criticizing or accusing you. But if you stiffen up and become defensive, it is like squaring your chest to invite a blow. Instead, take a page from martial arts, where the ultimate skill is to know when to step aside and let your opponents' energy carry them forward and off-balance. Figuratively, you turn sideways and watch their emotions flow past you ("I guess you're pretty upset with me, Mom," or "I know you think I'm making a mistake, Dad").

Pleasant smiles and compassionate nods keep you slippery, as well as centered and observant. A good thing to say in an especially tight spot might be something like, "That may be true, Mom. You might be right. I just have to do the best I can with what I've got."

3. Lead the Interaction

When you are interacting with EIPs, parents or otherwise, you are dealing with people who are lacking in flexibility, empathy, and frustration tolerance. They try to dominate using a few fixed defenses, which can include much control, criticism, and negativity. But their emotional over-reactivity also gives you the opportunity to lead the interaction to your preferred outcome.

For instance, in conversations with EIPs, they usually talk about things in a stereotyped and self-focused way, holding the floor with topics that matter only to them. Have you ever noticed how few topics they offer in a conversation? Have you ever noticed how rarely they ask about you? They are not interested in discovery or learning more about others. You can lead the way to a less boring experience by enriching the conversation.

You can steer and deepen the conversation. If you grew up with an EI parent, you may never have learned how to step in and steer conversations toward a more congenial topic. As a child, it felt like your role was to be the audience for whatever they wanted to talk about.

But now as an adult, you can take a leadership role in the conversation. You can change a topic, redirect a negative line of thought, soften a fear, or derail an oration by asking questions that alter the conversational path. By being ready to nudge conversations in a different direction, you can create interactions that feel more positively engaging to you.

You could express curiosity by asking questions like, "What experiences have you had that made you feel that way? How do you think things would be better if this happened? What might be some downsides to that? I wonder what unintended consequences that might bring. Any ideas?"

You could also encourage a more thoughtful conversation by saying, "Some people wouldn't agree with that. They'd say... How would you respond to that?" They still talk, but you've now made the conversation more complex and interesting instead of being dragged along passively. Being active in an interaction where the EIP tries to dominate you into a passive role is inherently self-affirming.

You can introduce broader topics. Because EIPs think in stereotyped ways, they get stuck in conversational ruts they can't shift out of, even if they wanted to. The rigidity of their self-absorption limits their topics. They may secretly welcome someone leading them out of the blind canyons of their own preoccupations.

You can ask about favorite TV shows and movies and what they liked about them. Inquire into best places they've found to buy things, food preferences, and virtually anything else in an area of their interest. You're not selling out; you're directing the show. You are deliberately staying active, instead of slipping into passivity and dissociation.

After EIPs have talked for a while, you can change focus by interjecting, "I have an idea about that" and then *briefly* share your thought, followed by, "And what do you think?" If this sounds like elementary, clunky conversation building, that's exactly what it is. But it's not something they're good at doing on their own.

It's often hard to come up with conversational shifts on the spot, so come prepared in advance with topics. A great idea is to use a game like Table Topics and pick out a few suitable topic cards to have in your pocket for the visit. They'll help you think of ways to break that mind-numbing EIP trance as soon as you feel it coming on. Questions about family history, questions about childhoods (yours or theirs), and questions about little-known relatives also could be interesting and may even be something you'll later be glad you asked about.

When the EIP is holding forth on something that you are tired of hearing about, you can interrupt and say, "Forgive me for interrupting, I know this is a little off the subject, but I always wanted to ask you…" And then be prepared with a couple of questions about them or their history you'd really like to know. Actively inviting other people into the discussion is another way to give yourself a breather from the EIP's monopoly.

In these ways, you actively lead the interaction into a livelier and more reciprocal place. They may not listen to your opinion, but you will be much more likely to be heard if you have *questions*. Again, the goal is not to change them, but to have more fun *leading* the interactions in ways that make them more interesting and engaging to you.

Leading an interaction doesn't overpower anyone; it just guides people onto a productive path. We wouldn't allow our kids to get away with monopolizing every conversation or always deciding what every topic should be. Similarly, it's not good for EIPs to be granted that kind of exclusive and unreasonable social power.

4. Create Space for Yourself: Disengage, Set Limits, or Leave

Before spending any time with an EI parent or other EIP, you should plan how you are going to create some healthy room for yourself. This is necessary so you don't disconnect from yourself or feel stuck in their one-person show.

Ways to Disengage and Keep Distance

Sometimes conversation is the last thing you want to encourage with an EIP. You may prefer to keep emotional distance because the EIP likes to engage in domination, criticism, shaming, or sarcasm.

Use fantasy. A friend of mine found that things always went better when she took a moment to imagine an impenetrable glass bell jar all around her before she walked in her mother's front door. Anything negative her mother said, my friend pictured her words hitting like pebbles and bouncing harmlessly off the glass.

She also amused herself during the visit by playfully translating her mother's criticisms into what she would have *liked* to hear instead, an idea she got from a funny video (Degeneres 2017). For instance, when her mother greeted her with a disapproving comment on her appearance ("Why did you cut your hair?"), my friend pretended she said something wonderful, like, "I'm so glad you're here! What a joy to see you!" The contrast made my friend laugh to herself, which made everything feel lighter.

Use compliments. Compliments were another way my friend created a more amiable space between herself and her mother. Although compliments don't seem like a form of disengagement, they certainly can be. Compliments put you in charge of the interaction and manage the EIP's mood marvelously. A compliment can be about anything the EIP is proud of. The best thing is that the EIP can then emotionally feed off the compliment instead of feeding off you.

Act fast. When you feel the need for some breathing room, it's important to act fast. If you don't take a break as soon as you start to feel fatigued or antsy, you can drift into their EIRS trance zone and be unable to extricate yourself for a long time.

If you are visiting with EIPs and you begin to feel trapped or drained by them, interrupt the interaction right away and say something like, "Oh, you know what, excuse me; I need to use the bathroom," "Well, I think it's about time for me to get a nap," or "Hey, I'm sorry, but I'm getting sleepy; I need to get some fresh air. I'll be back in a little bit."

Notice in these examples that you interrupt their stream of talk with an introductory word like "oh," "hey," "well," or "you know." These little words constitute the thin edge of the wedge you are driving into their takeover monologue.

Later as you become more skilled in redirecting conversations, you may not feel the need to escape with these kinds of excuses. But when you're just starting to create space for yourself, these are great ways of getting yourself back in the driver's seat. Once you've created some room for yourself, maintain space until you feel in control of the interaction and no longer trapped.

Make Sure You Have a Place to Retreat To

It's usually not a good idea to stay at the home of an EIP if you can afford not to. When you spend time with EIPs, you feel an odd combination of being simultaneously disregarded yet drained. Staying in touch with yourself around such people can be tiring because they relate to you like an audience, not a person.

Because EIPs can deplete you, having a retreat place and planning rejuvenating breaks are imperative during even short visits. Staying in a hotel or bed-and-breakfast can be the perfect way to have some family time while not turning yourself over to them for a full twenty-four hours. Telling them you have stuff to do for work also works well.

Having a retreat is essential because it gives you control of your exposure to them ("Dad, this has been great, but I think I need to go back to the hotel for a rest before dinner"). The EIP can't really argue with a physical need, and it makes far more sense to them than if you had tried to explain how their behavior makes you feel.

For example, whenever James attended family reunions out of state, he made sure to plan daily walks, drives in the country, movies, and shopping trips with his partner so they could get away from the family dynamics and decompress. They looked for the humor in his relatives' behavior and joked about the situation to keep things in perspective. They sneaked eye contact whenever someone did something particularly insensitive, knowing they could gossip about it later. Emotional coercion can't take hold if you don't take it seriously and give yourself frequent breaks.

Another woman texted her best friend frequently whenever she visited her family. Every chance she got, she stepped away and texted her friend with full emoji humor about what just happened. When her father complained that she was always on that damn phone, she laughed and said, "I know, I'm terrible about that!"

I suppose someone could say that these subterfuges are not aboveboard and don't contribute to an honest relationship. But before you can work on a more authentic relationship, you first have to be able to protect yourself in a more active, conscious way. In chapter 10, we will look at ways to be more real with EIPs, but it's best to learn some self-protective measures first.

Limit Your Length of Exposure to EIPs

No matter how much time or attention you give to an EIP, they'll think it's never enough. If you left it up to them, you'd be emotionally exhausted by the time they wind down.

Decide in advance how much exposure to them you can handle before you start zoning out. When that time is up, stretch your arms, give a big forced yawn, and say, "I'm sorry but I'm fading. I'd better get going," or "I need to stretch my legs." Then get up. Patting their hand or giving a little shoulder squeeze keeps things friendly, if that would feel comfortable to you.

If they complain or wonder why you're always so tired, you can say, "I know, right? Maybe I have sleep apnea." The fact is, being around self-preoccupied and emotionally oblivious EIPs *is* tiring. You probably do feel like a nap at that point. It's only fair: if they get to talk, you get to rest.

EIPs have no idea how long they talk or at whose expense. For example, Michelle dreaded phone calls from her old college roommate, with whom she no longer had much in common. After listening to her for a long time, Michelle brought the conversation to a close. Her roommate seemed surprised, and said, "Oh, but I could talk to you all day!" Michelle thought to herself, "Yes, that's because you're doing all the talking." Another woman reported that when she told her mom she had to go after an hour on the phone, her mother protested, "You *never* have time to talk!"

If you get calls from an EIP who goes on and on, voicemail is a self-protective solution. Responding to phone calls by text or email ("Missed your call. What's up?") is another way of keeping contact time-limited and to the point. People don't have the right to access you any time it suits them. You can return a call when it's convenient to you—preferably when you soon have to be somewhere else.

When an EI parent or EIP uses your ear as a dumping ground for their unhappiness or complaints, you can say, "Oh, you're having a hard time. Listen, I'll call you later when you're feeling better." Remember, it doesn't have to make sense; it just has to get you off the hook. If the EIP becomes accusatory or argumentative with you, you can say noncommittally, "Oh. I didn't know that," or "I hear you. We're different, and that's okay. I'm gonna let you go now."

It's a good idea to set limits when you first pick up the phone: "Oh, hey bro. Nice to hear from you. I got about ten minutes. What's up?" If the EIP tries to guilt you by saying something like, "You're always in a hurry. We never get to talk anymore," the proper response is, "I have ten minutes now. What's up?"

By the way, the phrase "What's up?" cues a person to get to the point, instead of encouraging longer responses by asking solicitous, open-ended questions such as, "What's going on?" or "What did you want to tell me?" This is not being rude; it is actually polite to let a person know up front what you have time for.

You Can Refuse Certain Topics

Lexi hated it when her mother, Joanne, talked about other family members. One day Lexi told Joanne she would no longer listen to gossip about them. Joanne was offended and defensive, and told Lexi, "Well, if I can't tell you, who else can I talk to?" Lexi realized this was not her problem to solve and told Joanne she would be happy to have conversations on other topics. After that, whenever Joanne started complaining about the relatives, Lexi broke in, said, "Gotta go, Mom," and hung up without further explanation. Sometimes Lexi just hung up or pretended the connection was breaking up. After a while, her mother would start to complain, and then say, "Oh yeah, you won't talk about this..." before going on to something else. This was another example of how effective persistence can be with EIPs.

Use a Style That Works for You

Lexi gave herself permission to call a halt and get off the phone *abruptly*. No long good-byes, no gentle wind-downs. She just hung up. On the other hand, Audrey was a person who felt more comfortable being nicer. For instance, when Audrey felt drained by her mother, she broke in and said in a kind voice, "Mom, I'm as sorry as I can be, but I need to go now. I'll talk to you later."

Abruptly or kindly, both women were successfully safeguarding their energy and declining their mother's control. Both Lexi and Audrey accomplished their goal of getting off the phone, but they did it in their own ways.

Abrupt endings may seem rude or mean, but they aren't. The EIP's lack of empathy makes them oblivious to more roundabout signals that you have had enough. You have just as much right to end the conversation as they have to continue it. Plus, you'll feel much more like listening later if you know you can end it whenever you want. Your limit is a good thing for the relationship. It's all part of being an active participant rather than a passive audience.

Just Leave

Most adult children have been trained to wait until an EI parent is finished with the interaction or else risk being called impolite or disrespectful. EI parents often refuse to let their children have emotional space. ("Look at me when I'm talking to you!") The child is certainly not allowed to say when they've had enough. This is part of the passivity training that children of EIPs get. They are supposed to stay put—perhaps dissociate—until the EIP is finished. In situations where an EIP won't give you room to say when you've had enough, leaving is not cowardice or rudeness. It is just another way of setting a boundary in a way that hurts no one.

Unless we are a physical prisoner, we can always leave, and it doesn't have to be socially graceful. In fact, it doesn't hurt to cultivate a little unpredictability that way.

————Sam's Method————

Sam trained his family to expect that he would come late and leave early. He was in a good humor while he visited, but then he would suddenly stand up from the table and say, "Well, this has been great, but I gotta get going," followed by a friendly hand wave and "Bye, everybody!" Sam found that he actually enjoyed his visits more once he knew he could leave when he was ready.

When he first started doing this, his startled family members demanded to know why he had to leave so soon. He used to offer excuses like, "I'm really beat," or "I ate too much." After a while, he stopped the excuses and just said good-bye. He didn't treat it like a big deal, and because he stayed in good humor as he did it, his family eventually accepted it. If they ever complained about his being late, he agreed, saying, "I know, I'm late for everything." After a while, his family just rolled their eyes as he left, and someone usually remarked, "That's Sam."

You Can Cut Off Contact

If EI parents won't respect boundaries or are too harmful in their behaviors, you can choose to cut off contact for as long as you need to. Sometimes we need a break from EIPs or parents who have become too draining or toxic (Forward 1989). If interactions are invariably painful, keep some distance until you feel strong enough to not be dragged down by them. When EIPs have been abusive, keeping distance might be the only option that feels protected enough. In rare cases, for good reasons, some people decide to break off contact altogether.

Estrangement takes a toll, however, so you have to weigh the costs of separation. The goal of taking a break is to get stronger so that even if you have some contact, you can stay free of their takeovers and dominance. If you decide to have only limited contact, very brief calls, emails, texts, or short visits may be all that can be managed for a long time.

When considering cutting off contact, ask yourself whether you might regret it later. That is the real test to base your decision on. Sometimes contact is just too painful. Sometimes the best possible relationship you can have is from a distance.

5. Stop Them

Let's look at what to do when EIPs act abusively. If their behavior is disrespectful but not an actual safety threat, you can be ready with a new "rule." Knowing their typical kind of disrespectful behavior, you can rehearse your planned response until it reaches the speed of an impulse. Abusive behavior catches most people by surprise, so if you're not ready with a response, you might freeze into paralysis. Responding immediately also has the element of surprise, which breaks up the EIP's intent to over-power. You stop them and declare the rules for future interactions.

Let's look at an example of limit-setting with a bullying parent who was *not* likely to escalate into further violence.

————Lisa's Story————

Lisa continued to invite her parents for family holidays in spite of her father's short temper. Then one Thanksgiving, her father slapped the back of her eight-year-old son's head for taking treats from the pantry without asking permission. Lisa saw red as she experienced a flashback of her own abuse. She shouted at her father, "Dad! I swear, if you ever do that again, you'll never see us again!" She could also have said something like, "Dad! We don't hit in this house. If you do that again, you won't be invited back. Tell Bobby you're sorry."

Lisa's strong reaction was necessary for setting a limit with a father who not only thought he was entitled to rule his own roost, but everyone else's as well. Lisa would've been within her rights to tell her parents it was time for them to go home. However, if Lisa feared real violence by her father, she should not confront him. Instead, she should try to de-escalate things and keep the situation safe, including privately calling the police if necessary. Later she could safely explain to him in a phone call or an email why she was not inviting them back.

Be Mindful of Safety When Dealing with Violent EIPs

With potentially violent EIPs, setting firm limits or demanding they stop may might things worse, depending on their emotional state in the moment. Standing up for yourself when someone is in a rage may endanger you. It's best to ask for advice from experts and follow your own intuition about how to best get through moments of danger in order to obtain a safe distance later. Your proper goal in such circumstances is to get through the situation without getting hurt. Once you're away from them, you can create a more comprehensive plan to keep yourself and others safe.

Respond in the Moment the Best Way You Know How

Sometimes EIPs endanger others because they lose emotional control, such as breaking things or driving a car while upset. This feels like being held hostage because anything you do could make things worse.

Sometimes in such situations, all you can do is breathe, stay aware, try to soothe the EIP, and look for opportunities to calm things down or get out of the situation. This doesn't mean you are weak; it means you are dealing with a dangerous situation in the only way you can.

However, you can plan what you will do in the future. You could agree to meet with them only in public spaces or always arrange for your own transportation. If they ask you why, tell them.

Your skill with these methods will grow steadily as you practice. You will become increasingly authentic and free from emotional coercion. After a while, you will feel a peaceful strength growing inside. To make these changes stick, keep encouraging and praising yourself for remaining aware and being able to spot emotional coercion before it works its way into you.

Highlights to Remember

You have the right to decline being taken over by EIPs. Any frustration caused by EIPs can be used as a signal to switch gears and think about the outcome *you* want. Take your time and create room for yourself instead of feeling pushed by the EIP to react immediately. Effective methods of side-stepping, disengaging, leading, and setting limits can stop their emotional control attempts. Watch out for your safety with potentially violent EIPs, and get expert advice for how to respond if they become abusive.

Chapter 6

EI Parents Are Hostile Toward Your Inner World

How to Defend Your Right to Your Innermost Experiences

It's hard to be yourself with EI parents. Some children of EI parents act out their distress by defying their parent, but if you are a thinker and internalize things, you may be more self-inhibiting. Around your parents, you may hide your individuality a bit and interact in ways that keep things smooth between you. You may always feel a little nervous around your EI parent, censoring and thinking twice before you speak.

What makes you so cautious about expressing yourself? It's because EIPs are so quick to judge and ridicule other people's inner experiences. To them, your inner world is unnecessary, a needless distraction from what they consider important. They expect you to agree with them, so whenever you express a different opinion or say how you feel, they take it as disrespectful. They act as if anything going on inside you has no merit unless they approve.

In this chapter, we are going to see how EI parents' hostile attitude toward your inner world can teach you to mistrust and even feel ashamed of your inner experiences, thereby undermining your self-confidence. EIPs instinctively don't want you to rely on your inner guidance because then you'll be much harder to control. Our goal here is to see through their demoralizing judgments to support your own feelings and point of view.

The Importance of Your Inner World and What It Gives You

Let's look at why your inner world is so important. There are five crucial gifts that come from your inner world.

1. Your inner stability and resilience

2. Your sense of wholeness and self-confidence

3. Your capacity for intimate relationships with others

4. Your ability to self-protect

5. Your awareness of your life's purpose

1. Your Inner Stability and Resilience

Your inner, psychological world develops in predictable stages, just like your body. We all start out undeveloped, then gradually form integrated, dynamic personality structures. If inner development goes well, your psychological functions weave into a stable cross-connected organization that allows different aspects of yourself—mind and heart—to work together seamlessly. You develop enough inner complexity to make you resilient and adaptable. You get to know yourself and your emotions; your thoughts are flexible yet organized. You become self-aware.

This is very different from the black-and-white, rigid, and often contradictory personality of the EIP. The inner world of EI personalities is not well enough developed or integrated to produce reliable stability, resilience, or self-awareness.

2. Your Sense of Wholeness and Self-Confidence

When you know your own thoughts and are deeply in touch with your inner world, you gain a sense of inner wholeness and completeness that increases your sense of security. Your inner wholeness also gives you dignity and integrity, and anchors you whenever you face stress or discord. It also gives you confidence that your feelings have meaning and that your instinctual guidance can be trusted.

3. Your Capacity for Intimate Relationships with Others

Emotional self-awareness allows you to share emotionally intimate relationships with others. The better you know yourself, the more compassionately you will feel toward other people. Real intimacy is a shared understanding of each other's inner experiences. Otherwise, it's just two people bouncing their needs and impulses off each other. Self-awareness also helps you select friends and partners who will support you and what you value in life.

4. Your Ability to Self-Protect

The ability to sense danger in your surroundings or untrustworthiness in other people depends on how well you listen to your gut feelings. To detect threat, you have to be aware of how situations and interactions make you feel. The primal instincts of the inner world are crucial to your safety.

5. Your Awareness of Your Life's Purpose

A good relationship with your inner world reveals what's meaningful to you and directs your life's purpose. If you don't form that trusting relationship with your inner world, you will be dependent on whatever your peers, the culture, or authorities tell you to be. In part II of this book, you will learn more specific ways to get to know your inner world and how to engage in this process more deeply.

EIPs' Attitudes Toward Your Inner World

Now let's look at how EIPs view your inner world. Understanding EI parents' attitudes toward your inner experiences will help you trust yourself instead of deferring to them.

They See You as Still Needing Their Direction

EI parents see their adult children as still immature inside, as if you were still their child. Seeing you in this outdated way, it's no wonder they keep telling you how to be instead of finding out what's really going on inside you. They feel entitled to assert parental authority long after you've become an adult.

Your adult inner world of feelings and opinions challenge their belief that you still need their input and direction. They may preach, criticize, or tell you what to do because they don't like the idea that you're now your own person. Ignoring your inner world helps them maintain the old parent-child relationship they are most comfortable with.

They Lack Curiosity About Your Subjective Experience

Because EI parents want to direct how other people should be, their child's inner experience isn't relevant to them. They think of children as empty boxes to be filled with what parents want them to know. Lacking in empathy and curiosity, what matters to them is how you treat them, not what you feel or think.

EI parents' disinterest in other people's inner experience explains why they don't listen very well. It doesn't occur to them that anything of much importance could be going on inside you, so they see no point in trying to grasp your point of view. Their dismissive attitude toward your inner subjective experience in childhood also teaches you to view your inner world as insignificant.

They Think Staying Busy Matters More Than Your Inner Life

To the EI parent, the important things happen in the outside world. They don't see why children should be encouraged to become aware of their inner worlds. To them, the inner realm of thoughts and feelings seems vaguely subversive and certainly unproductive. They think it's best if kids stay busy and focused on activities and externals.

With such a dismissive attitude, EI parents are often unsupportive of activities that develop the inner world. Reading, daydreaming, or art for its own sake can seem like a waste of time to them. To the EIP, everything should result in a tangible payoff, or what's the point? Even their spirituality tends to be heavily structured and rule-bound, with strict limits on acceptable spiritual beliefs.

They Are Impatient with Thoughtful Decision Making

EIPs want quick results. Consequently, they don't encourage thoughtful decision making in their children. Their guidance often consists of rules and platitudes, or they might just tell you to do what makes you happy—terrible advice for many situations. For them, thoughtfully consulting your inner world is a source of distraction and delay rather than wisdom. Taking time to think also means you are more likely to come up with something they would not approve of.

They Undercut Your Decisions

Although EI parents see thoughtfulness as pointlessly dilatory, once you make your decision, they often shoot holes in it. This is one of those crazy-making incongruities of an EI parent. You should quickly make a decision, but it should be in agreement with them. Taking thoughtful action toward your own goals is evidence of your individuation from them, and that makes them insecure.

They Invalidate Your Dreams, Fantasy Life, and Aesthetic Sense

Fantasy, imagination, and aesthetics originate in the inner world, so many EI parents consider these functions a waste of time. EIPs often dismiss fantasy as pointless woolgathering. They fail to see its role as the essential precursor to invention and problem solving. It's ironic that EIPs disregard the benefit of imagination, because everything in the man-made world was first invented in someone's fantasy life.

EIPs can be especially contemptuous of other people's aesthetic sense of awe or beauty. When EI parents critique or make fun of what their children find beautiful or meaningful it can really hurt the child's self-esteem.

Here are two examples of spoiling a child's aesthetic experience. As a teenager, Mila saved her money and bought what she considered a fabulous faux-fur jacket to wear to school. When she wore it the first time, her mother laughed and told her she looked like a mangy bear. When Luke plastered his bedroom walls with posters of his favorite bands, his father told him the musicians looked like losers. Both Mila and Luke could never see their cherished objects quite the same way again.

Because kids fall in love with what they find beautiful and inspiring, such parental ridicule is devastating. When the child's deep attraction to a desirable thing is mocked, it shakes a child's emotional self-confidence. Over time, these children become alienated from their inner world and can suffer from demoralization, depression, emptiness, and even addictions.

They Mock Your Inner Experiences

If your feelings or opinions differ from an EIP's, they are likely to shame, ridicule, or tease you. EIPs are well known for mocking anyone's inner experience that doesn't match theirs. Their derision suggests you're naïve and don't know what's right to think.

Their mockery can be expressed in many ways, such as "Don't be ridiculous," "Don't be silly," or "That doesn't make any sense," all of which say your thoughts are not worth considering. A look or sigh can also send the message that you don't know what you're talking about or that your ideas are absurd. These put-downs sow the seeds of self-doubt and self-consciousness. *You start to feel embarrassed about your own thoughts.*

Why EIPs Are So Hostile Toward Your Inner World

Often EIPs don't just disagree with your ideas; they react contemptuously and angrily. When one fifty-year-old woman told her father she had voted for a candidate he opposed, he jabbed his forefinger at her and said, "Don't you ever do that again!" The intensity of his hostility suggested he was not only offended but also threatened by the fact that she had her own preferences.

Let's look more closely at why EIPs can become hostile and attacking when you express your unique thoughts and feelings.

Your Inner World Threatens Their Authority and Security

EIPs don't like your inner world because it interferes with their emotional takeovers and threatens their authority. Remember, EIPs seek emotional control over you so you'll prop up their self-esteem and emotional stability. No wonder they get upset when you turn your attention from worrying about them to having your own thoughts and plans instead.

Because many EIPs need to be dominant to feel secure in a relationship, they find your individuality alarming. They rightly sense that once you trust your inner experience, you may slip the collar of their control.

EI parents may also worry that expressing your individuality could threaten their social standing. If your EI parents grew up in a community in which a person's social status depended upon rigid conformity, they may fear that your uniqueness could lead to social shame for them.

Your Self-Connection May Remind Them of What They've Lost

Hearing about your hopes and dreams can remind them of their own disowned inner lives. They may mock and criticize you to keep emotional distance and avoid triggering their own painful memories.

Your hopes for the future may remind them of their own lost opportunities. For example, one EI father ridiculed his son's dreams of being an artist because it reminded him of his own thwarted ambitions. This father never got to follow his dreams because he had to drop out of school to help support the family. He couldn't stand to hear his eager son express his excitement; it was too painful a reminder of what he never got to do.

How You Learn to Turn Against Your Inner World

It's bad enough that EI parents invalidate your inner world, but you may also internalize their negative voices. As a result, you could start dismissing your inner experiences and treating yourself with contempt. Here are some self-betrayals to look out for.

You Turn Against Your Inner Experiences

EI parents may be dismissive, but it's especially harmful when *you* turn against your own thoughts and feelings. As you reject your inner experiences, it will feel like other people wouldn't want to listen to you either. This is because you have adopted contempt for your deepest feelings. Once you side with an EI parent's disdain for your inner world, it's like putting yourself into emotional solitary confinement. Self-neglect and self-criticism take over.

You don't have to do this to yourself. Instead of scolding yourself with, *I shouldn't feel this way,* you could think, *I'm having this feeling. I wonder why?* Every time you accept your feelings and feel curiosity instead of self-rejection or shame, you are defending the idea that your inner world makes sense and should be listened to.

You Learn to Build a Facade and Become More Superficial

A child won't grow up feeling like a person of substance if parents aren't interested in what they feel or think. It's difficult for children to stay genuine when it feels like their parents are about to lose interest. To avoid feeling overlooked, many children build an impressive facade rather than expressing themselves honestly. As a result, they might often feel inauthentic with others.

Born out of emotional desperation, facades help manage how others see us so we don't feel ignored or judged. But even as the facade protects us, it makes our connections more superficial. Tragically, the more skillful our facade becomes, the more likely we are to hang out with cynical, judgmental people (because they live through a facade too).

If you sense you're living through a facade, try showing your true reactions a bit more. Ease up on the ideal self-image and turn your attention to what you're really feeling. Every bit of self-awareness diminishes superficiality. Every time you are a little more authentic, your loyalty to yourself increases. Your facade was probably the best you could do to win the approval of EI parents, but it may no longer serve you for optimal emotional closeness with others.

You Minimize Your Feelings and Shut Yourself Down

EI parents often react as if your normal emotions are too extreme, as if there were something wrong with you for having a heartfelt reaction. They thus teach you to downplay your feelings because they are uncomfortable with these strong emotions. They convince you that many of your emotions are unwarranted or excessive.

————Mia's Story————

When Mia felt sad or hurt as a child, her parents told her, "Don't be upset," or "You shouldn't feel that way." Yet, when Mia was really happy, excited, or looking forward to something, her parents would still warn her, "Don't get your hopes up." Their overall message to her was "Don't feel." Whatever Mia experienced, she always got the message that it was too much. Mild emotional arousal was all her parents considered acceptable. To avoid embarrassment, Mia learned to disconnect from her strongest emotions, whether positive or negative. This resulted in chronic depression as an adult.

"I think they wanted me to be happy," Mia told me, "but in a very shallow, let's-not-get-too-deep kind of way." Mia recalled that her parents accepted her happiness only about tangible, outerworld things *they* approved of, such as Christmas gifts, new clothes, or a good report card. Mia hid her true reactions because her parents often judged her feelings as excessive, weak, or oversensitive. Because of their rejection, Mia began to minimize and hide her feelings from herself too. She gradually lost her emotional freedom, her right to feel whatever she felt.

Fortunately, Mia reclaimed her right to her full emotional autonomy. She learned to stop playing it cool when she was excited or shrugging it off when she was deeply disappointed. She practiced staying open to her emotions and letting her feelings reach full form.

You can do the same. Don't kill off your true feelings. It's not right for you to feel fear and shame about feeling too much. You can reverse these self-betrayals by accepting your feelings just the way they want to be felt. The next time you feel excited, just let the feeling go through you uninterrupted. As an adult, you can let yourself experience your feelings in their unvarnished intensity. It's the best way to get to know yourself.

Unfortunately, if you've been made to feel foolish about your feelings, you may have learned to withdraw from people when you're upset. You may brush off others' sympathy by saying the equivalent of "I'm fine." But withdrawing from comforting is *very* bad for you because you biologically need it. Normal human beings are soothed by touch and emotional connection with other people (Porges 2011). A caring person's touch, voice tone, and proximity have a physically calming effect on us. Open yourself to this whenever you can. Don't give the message that you can handle your distress without any help. Appreciate people who show empathy to you, don't withdraw from them.

You Learn to Second-Guess Your Creativity and Problem-Solving Ability

The inner world is where all new ideas originate, so if you are self-accepting and playful with your thoughts, you will come up with more creative solutions. But once you are trained to doubt your inner world, your creativity and problem-solving ability will decline.

To reverse this, on your next tough problem, hold your mind open for new ideas and practice brainstorming without any self-criticism. When you are tempted to shoot down your ideas, keep asking yourself, "But what if I could? What might happen then?" Resolve to make ten mistakes for every good idea you get, and your mind will start talking to you again.

You Start Questioning Your Instincts for Happiness

Perhaps the saddest thing about dismissing your inner world is that you stop admitting to yourself what really makes you happy. Like Mia, you might become self-conscious about your joy and believe that a modulated response is more appropriate. You might even lose your sense of what's enjoyable and exhaust yourself with activities that are *supposed* to be fun.

However, once you reconnect with your inner world, you will naturally gravitate toward things that lift your spirits. By appreciating happiness when it occurs, you can amplify it and keep it going longer (Hanson 2013). By welcoming all your feelings, positive and negative, you reach out to yourself and feel more whole and less alone (O'Malley 2016).

How to Protect Your Right to Your Inner World

In this section, you'll gain some ideas about how to protect your inner world from an EIP's scorn. Your right to your inner world should be defended because in any relationship, *both* people have the right to have their inner experiences treated with respect. In fact, the idea of universal human rights is based on honoring the importance of people's inner experiences (United Nations 1948). Human rights defend people's rights to feel valuable and good *inside,* not just safe on the outside.

Let's look at ten responses to use when an EIP invalidates, mocks, or attacks your innermost experiences. All these responses defend your right to protect your inner world, by claiming your emotional autonomy and defending your right to self-expression. Once you give yourself permission to be loyal to your thoughts and feelings, you can respond in ways that change the whole interactional dynamic.

Response #1: Claim Your Right to Ignore Them

Sometimes not responding is the best way of responding. By ignoring them or moving your attention elsewhere, you put an end to their dismissal of your viewpoint. Ignoring is a great stopgap measure. Disregarding unwanted behavior is an effective way of decreasing its frequency.

Response #2: Suggest Other Ways to Connect

Sometimes EIPs mock or tease you because they don't know how to make contact any other way. For instance, at a family reunion Samantha's older brother, Rick, tried to connect as if they were both still in fifth grade. When he walked by her table, he thumped her on the head like he used to when they were kids.

Instead of accepting his behavior, Samantha got up from the table and followed him. Touching Rick on the arm, Samantha said, "If you're glad to see me, how about telling me that instead of hitting me on the head? That'd be much better."

Later when Rick overheard Samantha talking about her new car, he entered the conversation by asking, "What color is it?" "White," she replied. "Oh, like a toilet!" he said with a mischievous grin. When he made the crack about her car, Samantha looked thoughtful, then said: "I think you're trying to connect with me, Rick. I'm really happy about my new car. Do you have some *real* questions about it?" Rick was caught off guard, there was an uncomfortable silence, and then Samantha turned her attention to someone else.

Samantha no longer felt obliged to be a "good sport" about her brother's teasing. Whenever Rick tried to connect that way, she expressed her right to respectful treatment by not playing along. If Samantha had felt Rick was really trying to hurt her, she could've used more forceful responses. But she knew he was glad to see her; he just had no skills to say so.

Response #3: Use Questions to Block Their Disrespect

As Samantha demonstrated, using questions is a good way of letting disrespectful EIPs know that you won't participate in the banter of being teased. It interrupts old patterns and turns the attention back on them.

By questioning put-downs in a matter-of-fact—*not* challenging—tone, it makes the EIP's behavior stand out. Possible responses to teasing are "Now, what exactly are you saying?" "Could you tell me what you mean?" "I'm not sure I understand. Could you say that another way?" These questions should not be asked sarcastically, but calmly, with genuine curiosity. (Take a moment to practice saying these same three sentences in both hostile and curious tones to feel the difference.)

These questions show you heard the mocking subtext, but you're not going along with it. You're letting them know that if they are intending to put you down, they'll have to spell it out; you're not agreeing to read between the lines.

When exposed in this way, EIPs will often downplay their attacks by saying they're just joking or fooling around. To this, you could say, "Huh…I guess that seemed funny to you, but it didn't feel very good," or "Okay, I'll think about that. Maybe you didn't intend to make me feel bad." Whatever you say, you are clarifying their behavior instead of emotionally reacting. When you respond with neutral honesty and curiosity to a hostile swipe, there is no place for the interaction to go. Be ready to actively change topics after the awkward silence. It'll make both you and them feel better. Uncomfortable moments are a positive sign that old patterns have been interrupted.

Response #4: Deflect Instead of Reacting

Deflecting derails an unpleasant interaction by changing the tone. For instance, if someone tries to make you feel guilty or dominates you, you can deflect their negative energy by keeping things light and upbeat. You respond as if they had said something positive.

For instance, as Jayden was leaving to go to work, his father started lecturing him about wearing nicer clothes at his job. Jayden put a big smile on his face and kept repeating, "Bye, Dad! Love you, Dad!" as he picked up his things and went out the door. Jayden chose to deflect instead of feeling victimized.

Response #5: Roll Past Their Envious Putdowns

When EIPs feel envious of people, they often make fun of them. Here's an example. Alice had an important art opening in her parents' city. At the gallery reception, her mother introduced Alice to her friends as, "Here's my fancy-schmancy artist daughter!" Alice momentarily cringed: that was not how she saw herself and certainly not how she wanted to be introduced.

EIPs do this kind of attention-getting mockery in front of others so you feel like a terrible sport if you object. The most effective response to this behavior is to roll past it and hold on to your happiness. Alice defused her mother's jab by smiling and saying, "Yep, here I am!" as she shook their hands.

By responding with equanimity and humor, Alice didn't allow her mother to embarrass her or become the center of attention. By not reacting, Alice kept the focus on herself, where it should have been in a celebration of her success.

Response #6: Defend Your Right to Be Sensitive

When you express your feelings, EIPs often react as if you're overly sensitive and have no sense of proportion. After years of being told they make mountains out of molehills, many adult children of EI parents learn to preface their true feelings with "It's just that…" They anticipate humiliation, so they downplay the emotional importance of what they are about to say.

If an EIP says you are too sensitive and tells you not to take everything so personally, instead of feeling stung you could be curious and say, "Sure, what would be another way to take it?" or you could also clarify by saying, "Let me understand. You *don't* want me to take what you say to me personally?"

Another way to respond to "You're too sensitive" is to say with calm honesty, "Actually, I'm just sensitive enough." A deeper answer might be, "If I can't share my feelings with you, then I guess I've misunderstood the nature of our relationship." More simply, you could say, "Actually, I think mine was a fair reaction."

Response #7: Claim Your Right to Think Things Through

EIPs like to mock sensitive people as overthinkers who read too much into simple matters. They imply that you should accept whatever they say at face value without thinking too much. To the dismissive comment, "You think too much," my favorite response is, "I'll have to think about that." Or if you are in the mood for discussion, you could ask, "What did it seem I was overthinking about?" Or, to end the discussion, you could say things like, "Nope, I think just the right amount for me," "Well, I only think as much as I need to," or "Thinking pays off for me."

Because EIPs prefer emotional hit-and-runs, when you stop and clarify their intent in a deeper way, it makes you a less savory target for mockery in the future.

Response #8: Defend Your Right to Be Upset

EIPs are quick to point out how unnecessary your feelings are, especially if you're upset about something. EIPs like to complain a lot, but they have a way of making your problems seem like whining.

EIPs often "comfort" you by telling you to be grateful for what you have. This dismissal of your emotional experience is profoundly nonempathetic. Suggesting you could be grateful instead of upset sounds good, but it's not the way the mind works. Usually we feel better if we get sympathy, rather than being shamed for being upset.

As another example, if you were worried about your finances, an EIP might tell you to remember how lucky you are to have a job because a lot of people don't. Of course, this rationalizing does nothing but invalidate your feelings. Your neutral response could be something like, "I am grateful to have a job, but my financial problem's still there. It helps to talk this over with you. Is that okay with you?" This is a way of returning to the real point of the conversation instead of accepting their brush-off of your concerns.

Response #9: Defend the Legitimacy of Your Problems

EIPs like to point out that other people have lived through worse things. For instance, one woman's mother who was a war refugee as a child used to shut down her daughter's distress by saying, "What are you complaining about? You have three meals a day and nobody's trying to kill you." It's pointless to try to top something like that, but you could say, "I appreciate the life I have; I know others have it much worse. However, this is the problem I'm in the middle of right now. Would you rather I didn't tell you about it?"

Response #10: Validate Your Right to Feel the Way You Do

Sometimes EIPs flat out tell you, "You shouldn't feel that way," or "There's no need to get upset," thereby invalidating your experience. This suggests your emotions are wrong or abnormal. You can stay true to yourself by responding thoughtfully with something like, "I don't see why I can't have all my feelings about this." Or you could say, "I'll probably feel better later, but it makes sense that I would be upset right now." You could also challenge the implication that you're overreacting by asking, "Are you saying most people *wouldn't* be upset by this? Hmmm…I wonder."

Remember, the goal of the responses above is to stand up for the legitimacy of your inner world, not to try to change the EIP. Instead of reacting with frustrated passivity, you can take action and express your human right to feel your feelings and think your thoughts. When you speak up, you claim your status as a coequal.

In the next part of this book, you'll learn how to use your inner guidance, declutter your mind, and update your self-concept to reclaim your emotional autonomy and find the types of relationships you really want.

Highlights to Remember

We looked at how and why EIPs are often hostile toward your inner world. You saw how EI parents use mockery and other rejections to negate the importance of your inner life, teaching you to mistrust and invalidate your inner experiences. We explored the impact of EI parents on your relationship with your inner world. Finally, you learned ten ways to stand up for your rights to have your own feelings and point of view.

Part II

Emotional Autonomy

Reclaiming the Freedom to Be Yourself

In part II, you'll learn to pay attention to yourself instead of giving in to emotional coercions and fears of rejection. Instead of fearing the moods of an EIP, you'll protect your right to be yourself and to live your own life. You'll learn how to defend your emotional autonomy and mental freedom, allowing yourself to feel what you feel and think what you think. You'll stop denying your needs and build new skills to support your growth.

I am very excited about working with you to undo these patterns because I have seen it make such a difference with so many clients. I can't wait for you to enjoy what your inner world can bring you and how it can help you create your own best life.

Chapter 7

Nurturing Your Relationship with Yourself

How to Trust Your Inner World

Does it seem strange to think about spending time on developing a relationship with yourself? You might think, *I am always myself; why would I need to work on a relationship with myself? What would that even look like?* But it's the most foundational relationship you have; it determines your happiness, success, and genuine connection with other people. By getting to know yourself and valuing your inner experiences, you get better at understanding and loving others.

Unfortunately, you may have neglected your relationship with yourself as a result of growing up with EI parents who dismissed the importance of your inner world. This essential connection to yourself now needs—and deserves—some dedicated attention.

The Impact of Having Your Inner World Discounted

If EI parents invalidated or dismissed your inner experiences as a child, you may consider yourself unworthy of being taken seriously. You may even believe that what goes on inside you isn't important. I witness this often in psychotherapy sessions. Although clients come to therapy to talk about their problems, they often downplay their concerns with self-dismissive comments like, "I know this is stupid, but..." or "This is such a small thing, I'm embarrassed to admit it." Their interior world feels illegitimate to them, and they are embarrassed by their strong feelings. Take the case of my client Mallory.

———Mallory's Story———

Mallory came to see me after a corporate merger resulted in the loss of her position. She was ready for retirement, so the loss of income wasn't a threat, but the worst part was not knowing what to do with herself after she stopped working. Mallory had no hobbies or interests and no family that lived nearby. For the first time in her life, she had the freedom to do whatever she wanted, but she was drawing a complete blank. The thought of not knowing what to do every day terrified her. "I have nothing I'm really passionate about," she said.

Then one day, Mallory realized why she couldn't identify anything she loved to do besides work. She had had a very volatile and domineering father who loved to ridicule family members and tell them what to do. "All of a sudden it dawned on me," Mallory said, "that my father always put me down, he criticized and made fun of anything I liked or wanted to do." Even as an adult, he would discourage Mallory from trying new things, by saying, "You're too old. Why would you want to do that? You don't want to do that."

Once when ten-year-old Mallory was with her parents in a drugstore, her father caught her looking at a fan magazine. He called her mother over in his booming voice and said, "Look at what she's looking at! Look at this! Isn't that ridiculous?" Then he told her she didn't want that and whisked her away.

Mallory feared her father's scorn. "From the time I was little, his ridicule made this huge impact. I was afraid and embarrassed to voice my true desires. I lost all awareness of what they were. I never knew who I was. If he knew I wanted something, he told me it was trivial and stupid. I couldn't figure out why I didn't have passions or favorite things like other girls, but now I know."

"I learned to keep the part of me that was interested in things a secret. First, I was keeping the secret from him, but after so many years of feeling ashamed, I finally really didn't *know* what I wanted," Mallory explained. "When people asked me which thing I preferred, I could never tell. I would just say I didn't care because I was so afraid it wouldn't be the right thing." Mallory had been shamed out of trusting any cues from her inner self.

In adulthood, Mallory defied her father and became a successful, independent adult, able to be decisive and highly capable at work. But in the emotional areas of life, such as discovering her passions, she still felt repressed. She quickly shut herself down as soon as she felt curious or excited about something and wanted more. For a long time, she unconsciously chose her father's approval over her relationship with herself. Mallory had gotten so far away from herself she no longer knew what brought her joy.

When you repress your ideas and passions, your inner world shrinks. Many of us try to fill this vacuum of emotional self-neglect by obsessing over relationships and events. However, nothing in the outside world of people and situations will ever feel like enough as long as you dismiss your inner experiences. No amount of external activity can fill the emptiness where there should be a robust fascination with your own interior.

EI parents like Mallory's father can convince you that there's nothing about your inner world to take seriously. This self-betrayal lowers your self-worth and dims your joy in living. But it's a whole new day once you realize that your inner experience motivates your life and is crucial to pay attention to. In my years as a psychotherapist, I have witnessed many times the lightness, brightness, and feelings of freedom that occur when a person rediscovers the energy of their psychological interior. Diana Fosha (2000) calls these feelings the *core state*, and it's what is recovered if psychotherapy is successful. As one man put it, his new self-awareness felt like "finally getting over a wall." When I asked him what he found on the other side, he smiled and said, "The promised land."

But now let me play devil's advocate and ask, Who says that there really is an inner self, or that our inner experiences matter? How do we know the inner self deserves to be developed and trusted? As we have seen, EI parents are quick to ridicule the inner world, so what's the evidence that the inner world and inner self are real?

The Reality of Your Inner World: The Supporting Evidence

We popularly acknowledge the inner world all the time, relying on it for all aspects of living. We couldn't talk about human functioning at all if we didn't. We just don't realize how much of our daily life depends on consulting our inner world and our inner experiences.

Your inner world determines your most significant beliefs and decisions in life: who you think you are, what you believe in, and the future you desire. It inspires the kind of person you want to be, what you teach your kids, and the meaning of life. The inner world couldn't be more practical, because what's more basic than knowing what you need to survive and thrive? It is just as real as anything tangible.

When we talk about a person's confidence, will, and self-esteem, we act as if these qualities are real things, and they certainly are. So are trust, faith, optimism, and "going with your gut." Your inner world is the source of solving problems, having aha moments, and figuring out how things work.

Education is an example of an inner world pursuit that is highly valued. Your desire to educate and better yourself arises from your inside world, as do curiosity, ambition, and the ability to self-reflect. We could never set goals or envision something better unless there were an inner knowing guiding us forward. Somehow, we can look within, imagine plans, and chart a course in spite of external pressures and temptations. This inner ability to assess our lives and determine where we want to go is the force that allows us to change our lives for the better.

You couldn't be independent or make friends unless your inner self and inner world were real things. Your inner world is where all your energy, humor, enthusiasm, and altruism come from. Your ability to be fair and loyal to others comes from inside, as does any interest in coaching, leading, or mentoring. The desire to love others and better the world comes from the inside. The meaning of your life can only be found within.

Your inner world gives you resilience and the ability to work through hard times to eventual success. Common sense, compassion, and gratitude are inner gifts, as are adaptability and stoicism under hardship (Vaillant 1993). The inner strengths of patience, courage, and perseverance also are very real to us because we see them in action every day.

If you're still wondering whether these inner qualities really "exist" or should be considered "real," think what your life would be like without them. You can't, because not only are they real, but they are as essential to life as external events. Just because EIPs discount the importance of your inner world doesn't mean it's not crucial to living.

What Exactly Is Your Inner Self?

The idea of having an *inner self* can be hard to put into words, yet I've never had anyone look at me blankly when I mention it. All of us sense an inner core of ourselves that is unique and somewhat apart from everyday concerns. We feel its presence. Now let's define the inner self and what constitutes it.

Defining Your Inner Self

What I call the *inner self* has many common names: soul, spirit, heart, the *you* of you. Different theorists have used various terms to allude to this inner vitality: the *self* (Jung 1959; Kohut 1971), the *core state* (Fosha 2000), and the *true self* (Schwartz 1995), to name just a few.

I like the term *inner self* because it is simple, straightforward, and unmistakable in common parlance. When I refer to the self this way, people seem to know what I mean. The inner self is that internal witness— the nucleus of your being—that takes in all of life but is unchanged by life. The inner self is who you feel yourself to be at the deepest level. It's your unique individuality, underneath your personality, family role, and social identity.

Although you can't see, measure, or touch the inner self, you are internally supported by its presence and you'll have an empty feeling if you get disconnected from it. It's like a loyal and wise inner friend who always has your best interests at heart. It occupies your inner world and communicates with you through your inner experiences.

How You Benefit from Inner Self Guidance

Your inner self protects and enriches your life through the following sources of guidance.

1. *Emotions that alert you.* The inner self uses your deepest feelings—not just superficial reactions—to nudge you toward what's good for you. It energizes you when you encounter things that bring out the best in you, but makes you dread things that bring you boredom, dissatisfaction, or depression. It even warns you with apprehension, fear, or panic in potentially exploitative or dangerous situations.

2. *A sense of direct knowing.* Your inner self zeros in on the true nature of a situation or the intent of another person. There are some things you just *know* through your gut feelings. This intuitive knowing is what you mean when you say, "I see," "I get it," or otherwise grasp something all at once. EIPs may try to talk you out of this inner awareness, but the inner self knows what it knows.

3. *Inspired insights.* Inspired thoughts are different from the routine clutter of your daily thinking. Insights from the inner self deliver a deeper information than you would ever get from ordinary thought. When you are insightful, you reason clearly and see into the heart of a problem. Insights help you solve dilemmas, analyze cause and effect, and come up with creative ideas. Inspired insights often pop out of the blue while you're doing something else, such as walking, showering, or driving.

4. *Guidance for survival.* Physical survival may be the ultimate benefit of having a good relationship with your inner world. Exceptional survivors have had strong inner selves that they trusted and called upon under extreme duress (Bickel 2000; Huntford 1985; Simpson 1988). The rich inner worlds of successful survivors helped them survive, using the gifts of humor, altruism, imagination, meaning, and optimism (Frankl 1959; Siebert 1993; Vaillant 1993). As Lawrence Gonzales (2003) put it, "To survive, you must find yourself. Then it won't matter where you are" (167).

Exercise: Remembering Experiences of Inner Self Guidance

In your journal, write about a time when you listened to your inner self's guidance, using one or more of the prompts below. If you can't think of anything immediately, give it some time. Most of us have had these experiences at some point.

1. A time when you paid attention to your feelings, and you were right even though others didn't see it

2. A time when you instantly knew the right thing to do in a situation, even though you couldn't explain how you knew

3. A time when an insight or solution suddenly came to you after a period of not being able to figure it out

4. A time when intuition protected your safety or even survival

Your examples may be everyday or dramatic, but they are all evidence of this purposeful, intelligent guidance inside you.

Begin a Better Relationship with Yourself

As we saw in the previous chapter, EIPs dismiss your inner world as if it were unnecessary and irrelevant. If you believe these dismissals, you will miss the wisdom your inner self offers you in the form of feelings, intuitions, and insights. But you can use the following five ways to establish a more trusting, respectful relationship with your inner self and its guidance.

1. Pay attention to your internal physical sensations.

2. Figure out the meaning of your feelings.

3. Refuse to judge and criticize yourself.

4. Identify what you need.

5. Daydream about your life purpose and where you belong.

1. Pay Attention to Your Internal Physical Sensations

Like Mallory, you may have been raised to tell yourself things like, *That doesn't make any sense; that's crazy; I'm exaggerating; I shouldn't be feeling this way.* But sometimes physical sensations are more insistent. Your physical cues can give you a tremendous amount of valuable information about situations and other people.

One of the best ways to strengthen your inner guidance is to pay close attention to all physical sensations. Your inner self speaks through the body, with your well-being as its primary mission. Your body is constantly giving you a "state of the union" update, letting you know how your psychological and physical needs are being met, neglected, or threatened.

To build a better relationship with yourself, sometimes you have to relearn how to pay attention to your physical sensations. Many adult children of EI parents get so wrapped up in their thoughts that they can't feel their body's messages. They literally don't notice that they're tense, stressed, uncomfortable, or even afraid. Nor do they fully experience moments of joy because they have gotten out of touch with their feelings. With their hostility toward the inner world, EI parents tell you that paying attention to physical sensations is a waste of time. But they're wrong. Here are some physical cues that are excellent sources of guidance.

Pleasurable Sensations

When you're going in a good direction, you may feel a fullness, warmth, or blooming in your chest, along with a weight being lifted from your neck and shoulders. The world seems lighter, brighter, and freer, and so do you. You feel energized and have a sense of physical ease and capability, as if your body were ready to do anything. Psychotherapy researcher Diana Fosha (2000) has identified these core, uplifting experiences as times when transformative emotional healing is most likely to take place.

Physical Warnings

Your inner self also uses body sensations to warn you. For instance, a clenched stomach, tight neck and shoulders, an aching back, or tension in your arms might warn you when you're doing too much or are being subjugated. Or you might feel revulsion or skin-crawling in the presence of someone who wants to violate your boundaries. Sensations of fatigue, irritability, restlessness, and even nausea are additional ways your inner self tries to alert you to life-draining people and situations.

Energy Shifts

Your inner self reliably uses sensations of being energized or depleted to guide you. As you encounter certain people, situations, or even ideas, your energy level either rises or sinks. An increase in energy indicates you've found something enlivening to you. However, if your energy level sinks, chances are that situation or person is not good for you.

However, anxiety is the exception to this rule. If you grew up with EI parents, you might have learned to feel anxiety toward things that *are* good for you. For instance, if you grew up feeling ignored or rejected, you may have generalized that anxiety to all social situations. Fortunately, you can desensitize yourself to interpersonal anxiety by practicing repeated exposures to safe and welcoming people and social situations.

Depressed feelings also use energy levels to tell you when there's nothing in your current situation that is feeding the real you. It would seem almost unnecessary to mention this, but it's astounding how often we feel our energy level drop and yet proceed anyway because we tell ourselves it's the right thing to do. This usually turns out badly in the long run.

2. Figure Out the Meaning of Your Feelings

An EI parent's idea of sympathy is to tell their child there's no reason to feel bad. EI parents dismiss their children's feelings so much that often the child decides to cope alone. For instance, EI parents tell their frightened children, "There's nothing to be afraid of," rather than listening to what's frightening them. Just about the most self-alienating thing you can tell anyone is that there's no reason for what they're feeling.

When a parent teaches you to disregard your feelings, it's another way of telling you that your inner world doesn't count. This undermines your relationship with yourself. But rejected feelings don't go away; they go underground instead. If enough feelings are suppressed, they will ultimately come out in classic symptoms of depression, anxiety, or acting out.

Therefore, it always pays to look for the cause of your feelings. Trust that there's a reason and think about what happened just before you started feeling that way. When you treat your feelings like they make sense, you show your inner self that it can talk to you and you will listen.

3. Refuse to Judge and Criticize Yourself

Growing up with EI parents can make you very self-critical because they think that criticism is the only way to turn you into a responsible person. You end up feeling like you never measure up and constantly need to improve yourself. You evaluate yourself to a point that's destructive, not constructive.

Like your parents, you may think that self-criticism will make you a better person. But criticizing yourself won't improve you any more than attacking a child's self-esteem makes them more confident. Self-criticism is no way to have a relationship with yourself. It sentences you to a life of anxious dependency in which no power is greater than someone else's opinion of you.

Instead of judging yourself, why not think about what you'd like to change, figure out the steps to get there, and seek support? Even regrets about your past behavior don't have to turn into judgments. If you know what you wish you'd done differently, you've already learned your lesson and can forgive yourself in light of your new understanding.

Exercise: Expose Self-Criticism

Notice every time you think something derogatory or harsh toward yourself. How would it feel to hear that from another person? Pause to emotionally experience that self-criticism, and then write down how it feels. By catching yourself in mid-attack, you can immediately change it. For instance, "What a stupid thing to do!" could become, "I'll try not to do that again." Take pleasure in seeing how many of these old habits you can translate more positively.

---

4. Identify What You Need

When you are raised to put others first, you may lose touch with even your most basic physical needs, such as rest, sleep, or recreation. Early training in self-neglect means that it may now take a conscious, deliberate effort to take care of yourself.

EI parents can disrupt your awareness of healthy social needs as well because they often emotionally isolate their children for their own purposes. When you pay attention to your inner self's promptings, you might discover that you need more social contact, group activities, or community involvement than you thought. Fortunately, as you build a better relationship with yourself, you will feel increasingly confident and comfortable about seeking social situations you enjoy.

5. Daydream About Your Life Purpose and Where You Belong

EIPs are often skeptical and cynical about anyone's search for a more meaningful and rewarding life. Being so alienated from their own inner worlds, they don't see how daydreaming could ever be productive. But of course, daydreaming is essential to generating ideas for a more fulfilling life.

Your inner self urges you to daydream and imagine yourself in new circumstances that fit you better. You may not yet know your life's purpose or the kind of community you need, but once you start looking within, you'll feel more energized and hopeful. Daydreams are everybody's first step toward finding a more meaningful and rewarding life.

Value Your Inner Experience and Prioritize Your Self-Care

Adult children of EI parents often neglect their own self-protection and self-care because they've been told that goodness comes from putting others first. Perhaps you too may need to reconsider the value of your inner experiences in order to protect and take care of yourself. Following are five ways to prioritize yourself in your own life.

1. Determine Your Value

Have you ever sat down and actually made a decision about whether you and your feelings are valuable or not? Most people haven't. They might *feel* valuable or not valuable depending on circumstances, but they don't make up their mind about the worth of their inner experiences as a human being. EI parents don't encourage such self-appraisal because they want to tell you what's worth valuing. But this is an important decision for you to make because if you don't see your inner experiences as valuable, how will you be motivated to protect yourself or pay attention to your own ideas? How much you value yourself and your inner experiences determines what you will let yourself have in life.

Exercise: Do You Value Your Inner Experiences?

In order to have rewarding, reciprocal relationships, you first need to value your own inner experiences. If you don't find yourself interesting and important, you're not likely to seek someone who will. Use the following statements to clarify how much you value yourself. Answer spontaneously without overthinking it. Using a zero-to-ten-point scale, assign each statement a number, with zero meaning "I don't believe it at all" and ten meaning "I totally believe it and live it."

1. I am worth taking care of.

2. I am worth listening to.

3. I am worth understanding.

4. I am worth thinking about my needs first.

5. My feelings matter in every interaction.

By looking at your answers to these statements, you can see where you might be accepting dismissive treatment from others because you feel that way toward yourself. If you had low scores on any statement, it points to where you may need to develop a more supportive attitude toward yourself. If you detect a tendency in yourself to discount your inner world in any area, use that information to get back on your own side and build up a more loyal relationship with yourself.

---

2. Value Your Feelings Enough To Be Self-Protective

If you've ever cherished someone—especially a child—you know how you would feel if you saw them being mistreated. You would feel protective anger and a desire to help them. Can you feel the same way about yourself?

Many people don't feel entitled to self-protection and instead smolder in resentment. Unfortunately, resentment is a passive reaction and doesn't help you protect or care for yourself. Self-protective instincts can be scary at first because they come in the form of such strong feelings: indignation, outrage, or even hatred. But these are just emotional signals that someone has tried to control or dominate you. These feelings are telling you your inner experiences matter and must be protected.

3. Make Your Inner World Matter

Children learn their value by whether their parents attend to their inner worlds. You feel valuable to the extent that your inner experiences are respected and welcomed. Here's what to tell yourself for a supportive relationship with yourself.

1. *Your inner experiences count.* Show interest in your thoughts, feelings, and dreams.

2. *Your inner world is worth defending.* Be loyal to how you feel and protect your interests whenever you feel threatened.

3. *Your feelings and thoughts are just as important as theirs.* Put your self-care before other people's whims.

4. *Your mistakes are innocent.* Don't turn against yourself if you make a mistake and resist shaming yourself.

5. *Your inner world is worthy of being attended to.* Listen to your thoughts and feelings and take yourself completely seriously.

6. *You're worthy of spending time with.* Enjoy your own company and do things just because they give you a good feeling inside.

If you need more proof about the value of a good supportive relationship with your inner world, think about all the accomplished people who got that way by valuing their interests and giving deep attention to their inner experiences. We support that self-valuing in famous actors, Nobel scientists, great musicians, and world-renown artists. Nobody ever asks if such people should be paying so much attention to their inner world. We never question if it's okay for them to safeguard their time and energy from other people's demands. We should do no less for ourselves.

4. Prioritize Self-Care: Become a Good Parent to Yourself

Prioritizing your self-care is a great way of restoring a neglected relationship with yourself. Like a caring parent, you can support yourself for a life of thriving, not just surviving. You can appreciate and love yourself just for being alive. By cherishing yourself the way a loving parent would, you erase any old doubts about your value. By being loyal to yourself, you give yourself nonjudgmental, unconditional support and you commit to your self-development just as a devoted parent would.

By being a good parent to yourself, you reverse multigenerational traumas of low self-esteem and emotional self-neglect. You might be the first in your family to see the difference in life quality that honoring one's inner experiences can make.

Be a good parent to yourself and give self-support whenever you feel lonely, demoralized, overwhelmed, or tempted to be self-critical. Instead of just *thinking* supportive thoughts, try writing them down in your journal as you whisper or say them out loud. There's something about hearing support in your own voice that really helps.

Exercise: Comforting Yourself

Whenever you feel overwhelmed, afraid, or distressed, write down and say out loud every worry and feared outcome, no matter how insignificant. Express bluntly and simply what you're afraid might happen, just like a child would. Especially be on the lookout for the horror of being exposed as inadequate or bad (Duvinsky 2017). Just by admitting your fears and dreaded inadequacies, they become less terrifying. You might feel a little embarrassed writing down some of these fears, but don't let that stop you. It works.

When you've recorded all your fears, feel compassion toward that terrified and overwhelmed child self. Then write and talk to yourself as an empathetic parent would. First remind yourself that *everybody* feels overwhelmed at times and that it's *normal* to feel that way. Take your fears completely seriously, and reassure yourself that you are not alone and that you will get the help you need. Giving your inner child such comfort is an excellent way to become more self-accepting.

---

5. Find Emotional Renewal from Experiencing Your Inner World

Fortunately, the world today is much more receptive to inner-world activities, such as meditation, mindfulness, and journaling. Scientists have found health benefits, both physically and psychologically, in such practices that strengthen your relationship with your inner world. Interior-focused activities can lower your anxiety, bring you peace, and give you pleasurable awareness of just being alive. These practices insulate you from EI emotional takeovers and support the idea of honoring your inner life.

Mindfulness. You can practice mindfulness as you go about your daily life (Nhat Hanh 2011). All it requires is a willingness to stay in the present moment and become immersed in your immediate sensory perceptions. By doing this, you will feel the aliveness of being utterly present and aware.

Here's a mindfulness exercise to try. Take two minutes to perceive your hand as if you were seeing it for the first time. Notice everything you can about your hand: its outer shape, smell, texture, direction of lines, curves, shadows, and pale places. Find and squeeze its soft and hard areas, and feel its temperature. How many colors can you identify? Just keep noticing new aspects and experiencing its realness until your time is up. Notice how you feel afterward.

Meditation. Meditation helps you experience your inner world in a dedicated way that replenishes and relaxes your mind (Kornfield 2008). It has been proven to have many physical, mental, and emotional health benefits (Kabat-Zinn 1990). You could take meditation classes or use online meditation sites and apps (for example, Headspace or Insight Timer). Meditation involves sitting quietly with your eyes closed, relaxing your body, letting go of distractions, focusing on your breath, and letting thoughts float by without attaching to them. Meditation reveals that once you detach from the outer world, there is a spacious inner realm inside you that is uniquely alive and replenishing to experience. Meditation gives you direct confirmation of the inner world's reality.

Journaling. Writing down your thoughts, feelings, observations, and night dreams brings you closer to your inner experiences. Writers, scientists, travelers, and explorers have all used journaling to heighten their perceptions and refine their thinking. You could also use a book like *Mindful Dreaming* (Gordon 2007) to understand how your dreams can guide you in self-development.

Now that you've prioritized a better relationship with yourself, we'll next look at how to declutter your mind of false programming and update your self-concept.

Highlights to Remember

In order to nurture a good relationship with yourself, honor your inner world for what it contributes to your life. You may have neglected your inner experiences to satisfy EIPs' agendas, but now you can feel free to cherish your inner world as the source of your self-guidance and self-care. You can reverse any self-alienation by once again taking your internal cues seriously; deciding to value and protect yourself; and by improving your experiential connection with your inner world through mindfulness, meditation, and journaling.

Chapter 8

The Art of Mental Clearing

Making Room for Your Own Mind

If you grew up with EI parents, you may have been made to feel bad if your thoughts didn't agree with theirs. As a result, you might have learned to monitor your thoughts in their presence. Although you may now reject some of their beliefs, you may still be hyperaware of what they considered acceptable. But it is possible to separate your thoughts from EIPs' influence so your mind is once again free to work for you, serving your own interests and intentions. *Mental clearing* is the process by which you sort out which thoughts are really yours and which are hand-me-downs from others.

When your mind is your own, you are unafraid of other people's judgment and can think objectively. You can tell from a very deep place whether something makes sense or not. When your thinking is clear and validated by your inner experience, it cannot be seduced by false logic or guilt. With an independent mind and emotional autonomy, you can reason freely, even when EIPs insist on telling you what you should think. This ability to think clearly while considering your feelings and inner experiences is the essence of *emotional intelligence* (Goleman 1995).

Shame and Guilt Can Shut Down Free Thought

The freedom to think anything in the privacy of your mind is essential for your individuality and autonomy. Although EIPs might try to make you feel guilty, your thoughts alone can't hurt anybody else. Thought is an interior experience, not an interpersonal event. Thoughts innocently arise from our instincts for survival, security, and pleasure and are involuntary. They are the personal, raw materials of the mind and, as such, are neither good nor bad. However, EIPs judge your thinking to make sure you stay aligned with their beliefs.

————John's Story————

Although my client John was an effective professional at work, he had a hard time thinking clearly and decisively around his girlfriend. One day John realized why he kept censoring his preferences around his girlfriend:

"When I was growing up, not only did my true thoughts feel shameful, they never felt private to me. They felt dangerous to think because my parents had this little game where they would ask my thoughts on something and then judge them. My thoughts were only acceptable when they reflected my parents' beliefs. Otherwise, they were ridiculed as wrong, weird, or misguided. I tried not to share my thoughts with my parents because they would go immediately into judgment mode, like rubbing their chins and saying: 'Now, what do we think of this thought of John's?' I felt their verdict was either, 'This is a good thought; we approve,' or 'Your opinion is worth nothing, you idiot.'"

As John's example shows, you can be made to feel guilt and shame about your *thoughts* even if you haven't done anything to anybody. On the rare occasions in childhood when John did disagree with his mother, she stopped talking to him. He paid a heavy price for having his own opinions. "I was dead to her until I stopped thinking wrong," he said. It's hard to be clear on your own position if you know your opinion could lead to your being reviled. Because EI parents need to feel like they are right about everything, they make you feel rejected if your thinking doesn't match theirs.

As an adult, it's self-defeating to accept others' opinions instead of consulting your own mind. But EI parents teach you to do just that; they act like you're being rebellious or selfish if you don't consider them first in every step of your thought process.

EI Parents See Free Thought as Disloyal

For EI parents, everything is about how important, respected, and in control they feel. So what happens if you have your own thoughts and opinions? They see you as disloyal. To the all-or-nothing EIP's mind, your differing opinion means that you couldn't possibly love or respect them. Therefore, you may have learned to hide your more honest thoughts from your thin-skinned EI parents. Unfortunately, like John, you might have gone further and hidden your true thoughts from *yourself* as well so you wouldn't feel like a bad person.

When EI parents teach you in childhood that some ideas are forbidden, it can make you feel guilty about your thought process. Some of my clients remember how stung and ashamed they felt when their parents scolded them with, "Don't even think such a thing!" or "How dare you think that!" The message was that they were decent humans only if they saw things from the parents' point of view. Once EIPs convince you to start limiting and rejecting your own thoughts, their mind takes over yours.

But treating your thoughts as a test of your love and loyalty to other people is a misuse of your mind. When your first thought is, *Am I being loyal?* instead of, *What do I think about this?* you cannot think straight. Instead, you will cobble together incongruent rationalizations to fit EI relationship demands. Your emotionally coerced mind becomes preoccupied with monitoring your thoughts so as to avoid shame and protect other people's self-esteem and emotional security at all costs.

————Ashley's Story————

Ashley was depressed and exhausted trying to work a demanding sales job while responding to her elderly mother's frequent demands from assisted living. Her mother criticized Ashley for not calling her every day and not visiting enough. Ashley felt anger and resentment that her mother was so oblivious to her situation, but she didn't allow herself to set reasonable limits because her guilt-ridden mind kept saying, "I'm all she has." Ashley's mother was in a cheerful facility with an active social life, but Ashley irrationally accepted her mother's opinion that Ashley alone should be her first responder. Her mother's demands were like those of a toddler who pushes away other helpers and insists that Mommy or Daddy should do it.

Fortunately, Ashley cleared her mind enough to realize (1) she was not her mother's parent, (2) her mother was not in a position to dictate who met her needs, and (3) though she monitored her mother's overall care, she could not be at her beck and call while working a full-time job. This clarification of thought was a tremendous relief to her. Ashley also found she felt less resentful and more interested in her mother's care once she stopped feeling disloyal for even thinking about her own needs.

EI Parents Try to Tell You What to Think

Instead of respecting your right to think as an individual, EIPs believe they have the right to dictate your thoughts as much as they can. The diagram below shows how EIPs push their agenda into your headspace and leave you little room to think for yourself.

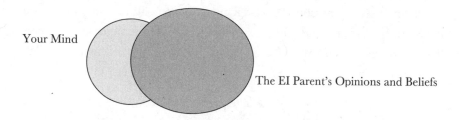

Your Mind

The EI Parent's Opinions and Beliefs

Your mind is the circle on the left.
The EI parent's opinions and beliefs are
represented by the circle on the right.

Picture the overlapped portion of the circle on the left as the part of your mind that has been overshadowed by the EIP's opinions. This overtaken section of your mind has been commandeered to the point where you now worry obsessively about how the EIP in your life will react to what you want to do. You can see how this mental takeover could cause problems in adulthood, as it did for both John and Ashley. You may find it hard to think for yourself when under EIP's pressure because you don't have your whole mind to think freely with, as shown in the image below.

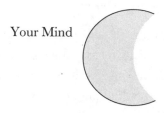

Your Mind

The area of your mind available for independent
thought, aside from EIP's pressure

This diminished mindspace is a big problem because creative thought depends on access to your whole mind, no matter where your next thought leads. Your creativity and problem-solving ability shrink when you start censoring thoughts that might offend or threaten an EIP in your life. To be a good problem solver, you can't limit your ideas just because they might upset an insecure person. However, once you separate your mind from EIP's control, your mind will spring back into its complete and independent form, as shown in the image below, allowing your ideas to circulate freely.

Your Whole Mind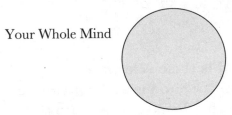

Exercise: What It's Like to Have Your Mind Limited

Look at the second illustration above—the mind crescent—then write in your journal how it would feel to limit your thinking to such a constricted space. Perhaps you can recall experiences like this when an EIP has dictated what you should think. If so, write those down too. How did it make you feel?

Respectful relationships depend on each person having the freedom of their own thoughts. The most satisfying relationships occur when you both can think your own thoughts and use your whole mind, without judging or correcting each other. In the diagram below, you can see how coequal minds can relate, resulting in sharing, not domination.

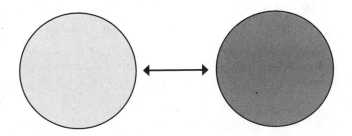

Two minds sharing thoughts without domination

Allowing yourself to accept all your thoughts is a huge first step toward being your own person. Just *thinking* freely for yourself is a significant sign of growth; you don't have to speak your mind to the EIP until you feel comfortable doing so. Later, you may communicate more of your thoughts to them in ways that feel natural and fit your personality. But there's no need to push it. Get your mind back first.

You Don't Have to Think Nice

Instead of teaching you to think, EI parents teach you to judge your thoughts. EI parents always turn thinking into a moral issue. They will attack their child's open, honest thoughts if they feel threatened. By acting wounded, insulted, or appalled, EI parents make it clear that you are only good when your thoughts are nice.

It's crucial to realize that you don't have to think nice. There are no thought police, thank goodness, and you have the absolute right to think anything that occurs to you. Your original thoughts are a big part of your individuality and are necessary to solve problems with creative thinking.

————Shelby's Story————

My client Shelby usually felt guilty for thinking anything "unkind" about her parents. However, to get her mind clear about them, Shelby wrote a *pretend* letter to them (never sent) about why she rarely contacted them anymore.

Dear Mom and Dad:

You wonder why I've kept my distance, but we can't have a reciprocal relationship when we're not equal. You've always been critical and judgmental toward me. Being around you has meant trauma for me. I don't even like you that much. You treat me like I'm stupid, but the fact is you can be so nasty at times, I'm actually unable to think in your presence. I don't feel safe with you. If I let you get me back in your net, I'll feel bad about myself and even worse about

145

you. You constantly tell me I'm not enough or "you're not doing that right." So I have every right to walk away from you because I haven't been treated well. I'm allowed to break away and find nice people I feel good with. You had no reason to make me feel so bad, just so that you could feel better.

Shelby felt relieved to record her true thoughts. You too can practice writing down what you really think, tolerating any anxious feelings that might come up. In this way you practice accepting your own mind. You never have to send it to anybody.

But What If They Know What I'm Thinking?

Children don't realize they have mental privacy. They believe others might read their mind and know their secret reactions. They take it literally when parents say things like, "I know what you're thinking," or "I've got eyes on the back of my head." Children can grow into adulthood still harboring an irrational fear that others will know if they think unkind things about them. But other people can't guess your thoughts unless you're showing it in your face or behavior. Con artists know this very well.

Children not only fear that their thoughts might be found out and punished, but they also don't want to hurt their parents. Children of EI parents are acutely aware of how emotionally vulnerable their parents are. It pains them to imagine how wounded their parents would be if their thoughts were known.

The remedy for this unnecessary fear of secret thoughts being known is to deliberately think freely in your EIP's presence. It may seem an odd thing to practice, but it can radically increase your sense of mental freedom. For instance, while listening to an EIP or EI parent, you might let yourself think things like, *That doesn't make any sense at all, You are treating me like I don't know anything,* or *I don't have to believe that.* By thinking your own thoughts, you push away their mental domination. You enjoy the fact that you can think whatever you want, and they will never know.

Is Magical Thinking Inhibiting Your Thoughts?

I've had many clients who've been hesitant to admit their honest thoughts because they secretly feared these thoughts might bring harm to others. This fear is left over from childhood, when we worried that our thoughts might come true. It can take years of maturation for children to realize that thoughts can't hurt anybody. Even some adults worry and "knock on wood" to avert bad outcomes from speaking certain thoughts.

If you still secretly fear the destructive power of your thoughts, remind yourself that many truly desperate people under the most extreme conditions—much worse than yours—have been powerless to make their most fervent wishes come true. You can't make things happen with your thoughts alone, and other people can't read your mind. It's coincidence if it seems that way.

Your freedom of thought is foundational to your psychological health and independence. No matter how "bad" some thoughts may seem, they're natural and blameless phenomena with a life of their own. The healthy human mind thinks without boundaries, so wise people let their thoughts come and go without taking much ownership of them. Sometimes thinking is a great way to blow off steam; it doesn't hurt anybody and can't be controlled anyway. We can choose our actions, but none of us has any choice about what we'll think next.

Thoughts Don't Make You Bad

Unfortunately, some say thoughts are as bad as actions, but I believe that is a misunderstanding of a moral lesson taken out of context. For instance, the teaching that thinking about something is as bad as doing it is *not* saying that fantasies are literally the same thing as actual behavior. It's simply a caution to think twice about holier-than-thou hypocrisy and judgment. We can't pretend that some ideas would never cross *our* mind because as a human being, of course they could. We have no control over what thoughts occur to us. It's only what you do with those thoughts that counts.

Separate Your Own Thoughts from the Clutter of Inherited Thoughts

If you grew up under pressure to think like your parents, you may now have to weed out their influence to discover which thoughts are truly yours. Which of your values come from your own conscience, and which have been mindlessly passed along to you? Which thoughts are gold, and which are clutter?

The process of mental clearing is very simple: mistrust any thought that gives you a sinking feeling. Many people think self-critical thoughts are the voice of their conscience, but that's not true. Legitimate conscience guides you; it doesn't make sweeping indictments of how good or bad you are. A healthy conscience supports moral growth by leading you to make corrections or offer amends. Harsh self-judgment and self-blame are mockeries of self-guidance, echoing the rigid thinking of EIPs in your childhood. Your conscience's proper role is as guide, not attacker.

Our true thoughts have a matter-of-fact, clear quality. They do what thoughts are supposed to do: help us solve problems, be creative, protect us, and get our needs met.

But inherited thought-patterns are different; they feel tyrannical. Their oppressive guilt tells you their roots started in early emotional coercion. It's not your natural mind that tells you to be perfect or beats you up for making mistakes. Nor does it tell you it's wrong to disagree with authorities no matter what. Pressured, self-attacking, or guilty thoughts are the mental legacy left behind after you've been emotionally overpowered by EI authority figures.

Here's what my client, Jasmine, had to say about the difference between her true thoughts and the internalized criticisms of her EI parents: "I've been hearing the critical voice lately and realizing it's not my voice. It's a voice I thought was mine, but now I'm separating myself from it and choosing something else. Now, when I hear a negative voice about myself, I realize it's not coming from me!"

When You Think "I Should" or "I Have To," Stop and Reconsider What You Want

Whenever you find yourself thinking, I *should*, or I *have to*, stop and ask yourself where you learned this rigid rule. Then ask yourself what your actual options are. That is what Ashley did in the earlier story. She realized that her "should" feeling was based on the belief that her mother's demands were more important than her own fatigue. She had inherited the belief that good children always put their parents first. Ashley felt much better once she rationally considered her limits and realized that catering to her mother's preferences wasn't a "should" she wanted to keep.

EIPs' "shoulds" tell you to be self-sacrificing and put them first, which would make sense if EIPs really were the most important people in the world. But because they're not, try asking yourself clarifying questions like: *Why am I feeling guilty and bad if I don't meet their expectations?* or *Is what they want respectful and reasonable for them to expect?* This will help you sort through the mental clutter and see the situation more fairly. As an adult, your job is to take care of your own emotional health, not try to win the approval of someone who may be thoughtlessly asking for more than you can comfortably give.

Early Emotional Takeovers Can Cause Depressive Thinking

Making children feel guilty or ashamed in childhood promotes feelings of immobilization and depressive thinking. However, you can sweep away these disempowering states by realizing their origins in past emotional coercions by EI parents. Once you label depressive thoughts for what they are and where they came from, you can replace them with more realistic, self-supportive thoughts that strengthen you.

In his book *Feeling Good*, psychiatrist David Burns (1980) analyzes how depressed people think and how to use cognitive self-therapy to transform depressing thoughts. Whatever the source of depression—physical or psychological—depressive thoughts are full of self-imposed coercions, as if you have no choice but to accept a life you don't particularly like. Many people's minds are littered with these extreme, all-or-nothing thoughts passed down by EI parents.

Burns recommends undoing depressive thoughts by deliberately thinking more assertive, reasonable, and flexible thoughts. The idea is to train your mind to immediately counter extreme or hopeless thoughts with reason and perspective, much like a defense attorney might cross-examine an opponent's witness (Burns 1980).

Burn's cognitive self-therapy is effective because it helps you spot the defeatist, unrealistic roots of your thinking and prompts you to change it *actively* and intentionally. Instead of listening to all your demoralizing thoughts as if they were facts, you can label them as negative thinking and contest their distorted view of life. You can reframe hopeless, critical, and discouraging thoughts into more realistic, hopeful ideas.

For instance, if you have a demoralized, exaggerated thought like, *I'll never finish this work,* stop yourself and think something more realistic like, *If I keep doing one piece at a time, this job will eventually be done.* If you think, *I really screwed that up; I can't do anything right,* stop and ask yourself whether that's really true (it's not), and then think more supportively, like, *I made a mistake because I was brave enough to try; now I can fix it and try something else.* If an upsetting event occurs, instead of thinking, *It's the end of the world; I'll never get over this,* you can say to yourself, *This is not the end of the world, but it is a huge shock. I will find a way to deal with this a little bit at a time.*

Anxiety and Worry Are Types of Mental Clutter

Mental clutter are thoughts that didn't originally belong to you. They cause feelings like shame, fear, obsessive worry, hopelessness, helplessness, pessimism, and self-criticism. I call these thoughts clutter because they were not originally a part of you and have nothing to do with the natural functioning of your mind. They just create disorder and distortion. Think of these thoughts as debris left over from EI parents' emotional coercions. EI parents often promote demoralized thinking in their children because it makes them easier to control.

It is important to distinguish whether your thoughts are your own or family hand-me-downs. Consider that some of your most anxious thoughts might be multigenerationally transferred fears, originally designed to protect a long-ago ancestor from a hostile environment. Think of these demoralizing and inhibiting thoughts as dusty, rickety furniture that has been passed down in the family for generations. Maybe it's up to you to be the first person to say you don't want it.

Obsessive worry is another type of thought that comes from being the child of EI parents. This comes about because these children have to be so hypervigilant to their parents' moods. When your emotional security feels threatened by a parent's upheaval, you learn to obsess over why someone is upset and what could happen as a result. You worry about what you should do to make things right for them.

Unfortunately, worrying about others' moods prevents you from focusing on how you feel and what you think. It would be much more productive to drop the worry and consider what it's like to be interacting with them. You could ask yourself, *How do I wish they'd treated me? How is this affecting me? Did I really deserve their behavior?* You then would be thinking freely and considering yourself as important as they are.

Whenever you find yourself obsessing over whether someone is unhappy with you, shift into your own viewpoint and write about how their behavior makes *you* feel. Get back in your own shoes and come up with your own opinion about the situation instead of accepting their criticisms at face value. Thinking your own thoughts lets you see what you want out of the situation, allowing you to plan the outcome you want. Using your mind in this active, purposeful way lets you pursue your own personal happiness instead of fruitlessly worrying about how to placate EIPs.

Self-Talk Is Your Ticket to Mental Clarity

Talking to yourself within the privacy of your mind is the primary way you can change your mood and thinking. You can use self-talk to specify your desires, come to grips with disappointment, and determine your goals. Just make sure what you are saying to yourself helps you focus on what you want and what really matters to you.

Constructive self-talk helps you guide yourself out of emotional domination. Just as an effective GPS voice shows the way, so can your inner voice. Self-talk helps you clarify your intentions and set desirable goals. If EIPs have subjected you to emotional takeovers by putting their interests ahead of yours, you can now reverse this by talking yourself through new responses and behaviors.

Self-Talk Makes It Impossible to Disconnect from Yourself

Self-talk is how you stay in touch with yourself when EIPs are trying to take over. Let's say you are visiting your parents, and they react negatively to something you do. This could trigger a childlike reaction, making you feel helpless and immobilized by their criticism. But if you are ready for such predictable domination from them, you could stand there, look them in the face, and still think your thoughts. You wouldn't be surprised by their behavior, nor would you renounce your adult mind and let them take over. You would just stay in touch with yourself and observe.

If others show disapproval, you could talk to yourself and remind yourself that you have the right to your own thoughts and desires. If they lay a guilt trip on you or criticize your values, you could remind yourself of your unassailable worth as a person. You would be able to stand firm in your own thoughts, regardless of what they were saying and know that their displeasure means nothing about your self-worth. Your self-talk is your bridge back to trusting and reconnecting with your real self.

Self-Talk Reverses Brainwashing

EI parents feel justified in trying to brainwash you into their point of view. They first shut down your rationality by getting you upset and defensive. Under these conditions, you become more vulnerable and ultimately susceptible to what they tell you to think.

To counteract an EIP's mental and emotional domination, you tell yourself to keep your analytic mind sharp. You can fight the urge to shut down and go foggy when they are upset with you. Instead, you can mentally narrate observations on their behavior, as if you were an anthropologist taking notes. This analytical self-talk will anchor you in the objective, adult part of your brain that can see through their attempts to control you.

As you accurately label their behavior with your self-talk, their attempts at emotional takeovers will fail. Maintaining loyalty to yourself and thinking analytically are exactly the skills that prisoners of war and other victims of totalitarian regimes use in order to hold on to their integrity and beliefs over years of abuse or imprisonment.

Three Situations for Practicing Self-Talk

Self-talk brings you emotional strength. However, self-talk can be hard to come up with on your own, so here are some suggested self-talk phrases to use when you feel pressured by the coercive expectations of an EIP.

1. When you feel blamed for not doing enough, tell yourself:

    I haven't done anything wrong. I can listen, but I won't accept guilt.

    I'm not bad, and this isn't all about me.

    It's not my fault she's disappointed. Her expectations were truly out of line.

    This will blow over, even if he's acting like nothing will ever be right again.

    She expects more than I can give. I would never be able to do all that, nor would I want to. What she wants me to do would stress and debilitate me.

2. When someone loses emotional control, say to yourself:

    It's not my fault that he can't manage his emotions.

    She's upset, but I'm still okay. The world is still turning.

He's doing his wrath-of-God act, but that doesn't mean he's right about this.

Someone being upset doesn't mean I have to let them dominate me.

What's she's saying is an overwrought exaggeration.

She's trying to convince me this incident is the end of the world. It simply isn't.

3. When someone tries to dominate you and control your thinking, remind yourself:

    My needs are just as legitimate and important as his. As adults, we're coequals.

    My life doesn't belong to her. I can disagree.

    I choose my loyalties; he doesn't get to claim my primary loyalty.

    My worth is not defined by how he feels toward me.

    These are just her opinions; she doesn't own me.

By using such self-talk during an interaction, you maintain a strong self-connection that can't be broken. Realistic self-talk helps you keep perspective, and reminds you that your inner world and needs are equally as important as the EIP's.

Once You Clear Your Mind, What Will You Fill the Space With?

Think of your mind as a box with only so much room for thoughts. If you increase one type of thought, there is less room for anything else. Overall, your goal is to focus on so many pleasant experiences that negative thought-patterns get crowded out.

Deliberately increasing time spent on thoughts of pleasure, enjoyment, and possibility changes the ratio of pleasurable to toxic thinking. When you accentuate and dwell on positive experiences, you become immune to EIPs who use fear, guilt, and shame to control your mind. Rick Hanson is a neuropsychologist whose book *Hardwiring Happiness* (2013) explains the brain benefits of amplifying our pleasurable, appreciative thoughts. He says that when you devote even a few seconds at a time to deliberately experiencing more happy thoughts, you can reconfigure your brain's habitual thought-patterns.

As Hanson explains, the more time you spend savoring your pleasurable experiences, the more you train your brain toward feel-good mental habits (Hanson 2013). It is no longer up to everybody else whether you have a good day or feel like a worthwhile person. By consciously focusing on what you like and value about yourself, you can intentionally change your mood.

Diana Fosha (2000) has shown that healing emotional transformations are most likely to occur while we are in an uplifted positive state, rather than when we focus on negative, self-critical experiences. The quest for self-knowledge and positive, self-affirming experiences is not escapism; it is what we need to change for the better.

By expanding and deepening your moments of happiness, you also strengthen your individuality and autonomy. When you deliberately recall the feelings of happy experiences, you are in control of your mood and self-esteem. All these little moments of intentionally savored happiness and self-approval increase feelings of self-efficacy. This adds up to a rewarding sense of yourself as an active, self-determined person—making you less susceptible to the emotional coercions, takeovers, and distortion fields of EI people.

The important thing is not just to think happier thoughts, but to bring up autonomous, guilt-free, and warm feelings inside. Once you discover that you can actively change your internal state just by focusing on what makes you feel better, you won't feel so dependent on unrewarding relationships. You will be able to create your own sense of efficacy, autonomy, and comforting experiences to increase your happiness.

Highlights to Remember

EIPs' emotional demands can make you feel guilty and ashamed for having your own thoughts, thus immobilizing your ability to think for yourself. Clearing your mind of thought-clutter accumulated from a parent's emotional takeovers will restore your mental freedom. "Should" thoughts can be challenged to help you avoid depressive thinking and make up your own mind. Accepting that your mind is safely private and that thoughts alone can't cause harm strengthens your freedom of thought. Self-talk also helps prevents self-disconnection and emotional takeovers in the moment. When you focus your thoughts on experiences that confirm your goodness and strengthen your happiness, you'll feel the pleasure of getting your mind back.

Chapter 9

Updating Your Self-Concept

How to Correct Distortions and Enhance Self-Confidence

Your self-concept is the basis of everything you believe about yourself and what you allow yourself to become. This understanding of yourself was impacted by how people treated you when you were growing up. Their behavior told you a story about who they thought you were. As a child, you had no choice but to learn about yourself through their eyes. But EI parents aren't much help in developing an accurate self-concept because they often overlook their children's unique qualities, capabilities, and interests.

EI parents expect you to grow up according to their assumptions. With parents like these, it's hard to know yourself in a way that reflects your strengths accurately. Instead, you might judge yourself only by how well you've met their expectations. Sadly, EI parents often discourage their children with negative feedback that makes them feel like less than they are. It's crucial to correct these erroneous self-beliefs so you can live more authentically, pursue your personal development, and deepen your connections with yourself and others.

EI parents disregard others' individuality, so they won't teach you much about yourself. They lump people together, seeing them as much more similar than they really are. Individual complexities are ignored as they say things like, "You're just like your father!" or "You're like my side of the family." They think they know you because you remind them of someone. As a result, they give you a typecast self-concept that doesn't really fit you. With EI parents, you were told what to be, not helped to discover who you are.

But now as an adult, you can expand your self-concept to include all your potential and complexity, even if EIPs still pigeonhole you in an over-simplified or childlike identity. You don't have to go through life feeling like less than you are. Thankfully, your self-concept no longer has to be held hostage by your parents' opinions. You are now free to discover who you are and what you want to become. You can update your self-concept to fit who you really are.

First, however, let's briefly explore the childhood emotional climate that influenced your concept of yourself. This will shed light on how you now see yourself, and help you free yourself from an outdated identity based on how you were treated as a child.

Exercise: Reviewing Your Childhood Self-Concept

Give yourself some time to think and use your journal to write down your answers to the following questions.

- What was your self-concept as a child?

- How did you see yourself around other children?

- Did your parents help you identify and develop your potential strengths?

- Did you have a clear identity, or were you just one of the kids?

- Did they encourage you to think ahead and imagine your best adult life?

- Did they ask you about the kind of impact you wanted to have on the world?

- Did they treat you like you going to be a successful and loving person?

Next, read over and reflect on what you wrote. What are your reactions? How do you think your childhood may have affected your self-concept in your adult life?

_____

The good news is that you now have the ability to counteract and repair negative childhood effects on your self-concept. If EI parents couldn't help you know yourself accurately in childhood, you can do it for yourself now in adulthood.

Make Sure You Protect Your Adult Self-Concept

As we've seen, EI parents see qualities in their children that serve the parents' needs. Therefore, you may have been told things about yourself in childhood that simply weren't true. But now as an adult, you can consciously build a more accurate and supportive self-concept.

This is especially important because as an adult how you see yourself affects every part of your life. Have you allowed yourself to grow into a self-affirming adulthood? If you don't see yourself as worthy, you won't take charge when you need to. If you don't find yourself interesting, how will you promote yourself or have close, rewarding relationships with others? If you aren't self-protective, how can you feel safe with anyone?

Now let's look at how to correct some adult distortions in self-concept that are caused by EI parents.

Realize You Are Now an Adult with Authority

Many EI parents never acknowledge their grown children as full adults. These parents undermine their adult children's dignity by making them feel silly or presumptuous for taking themselves seriously. Their adult children end up feeling sheepish about claiming their adult authority and independence. Without their parents' blessing to grow up and be their full equal, these adult children wear their adult authority uneasily.

—————Jonelle's Story—————

Jonelle loved her executive job and was good at it, but her assistant Todd slowed her productivity by asking unnecessary questions and talking about personal matters whenever he got the chance.

The need to set limits was obvious, but Jonelle felt sorry for Todd and tried to listen when he wanted to talk. In fact, she made it worse by often asking him how he was doing. She couldn't seem to stop herself, although she was already thinking about replacing Todd.

The real problem was that Jonelle didn't feel her adult authority. She still saw herself as the rescuer child in a family of five who comforted her unhappy and unfulfilled mother. This old self-concept showed through as she explained why she tolerated Todd: "It's because he has to stay behind in the office while I get to travel and have fun. I actually feel bad about being his boss and making so much more money than him. I feel bad about shutting him out; I want him to feel I'm available to him." The idea that Todd would be offended by his boss's requests or feel "shut out" was straight out of Jonelle's relationship with her mother.

However, once Jonelle realized that her outdated self-concept was undermining her success, she gave up the guilt, claimed her adult authority, and set appropriate limits with Todd.

Look at your own life now and see whether there are situations where you hesitate to assert your legitimate authority for fear of alienating someone. Fortunately, you can change this because it's within your power to overcome childhood influences and continue developing yourself (Vaillant 1993). Through your natural capabilities and mentoring from others, you can build a stronger self-concept and be an effective leader even if your parents didn't see you that way.

Know You Are Not an Imposter

The *imposter syndrome* (Clance and Imes 1978) makes it hard to fully own your accomplishment because it doesn't *feel* like it came from you. You secretly fear being exposed as a fraud, like a child playing dress-up. Yet the real problem may be that you haven't consciously updated your self-concept beyond who you were in childhood.

You might feel like an imposter in relationships as well, finding it hard to understand why others love you. For example, one woman was shocked when her friends surprised her with a big birthday party. She didn't feel important enough to be celebrated in this way and said, "I don't understand this, but thank you."

Many adult children are protective of their family members' narcissism and feel uncomfortable challenging their entitlement to center stage. Such adult children will downplay their success as soon as the spotlight hits them. Instead of feeling proud, they think, *This isn't really me.* They stop themselves from feeling successful because they feel bad for diverting attention from their egocentric family member.

The imposter sensation—obviously distorted because you *did* do the work, it *was* your party—makes perfect sense if you grew up believing you were not as interesting as a more entitled EI family member.

As an example of such entitlement, consider the father who attended his daughter's award ceremony, but sat there and steamed about how there were too many people, how it was taking all night, and how he was missing the ball game on TV. Then there was the mother who kept huffing about how unbelievably inconsiderate it was for the college to hold her son's graduation on Mother's Day weekend. These parents communicated that their comfort was much more important than their child's success.

Just because EIPs don't support your moments of success, it doesn't mean you have to discount your adult accomplishments. In fact, with parents like this, you need to be even more self-supportive. Don't be distracted when they try to hijack all the attention. Cherish every bit of your success and incorporate it into your self-concept.

Protect Your Adult Self from Your Parents' Distortions

EI parents look at their children through their own projections. As a result, they can give their children a warped image of who they are. Sometimes this distortion is nearly unbelievable.

For instance, Lily had struggled her entire adolescence from anorexia, abetted by her mother's pathological obsession about food and weight. Even when Lily was dangerously thin, her mother kept commenting on anything that could be a fattening food choice. Even after Lily had healed her self-image and regained a normal, healthy weight as an adult, visits home to her mother could reactivate her anorexic thinking. Her mother continued to make veiled comments about Lily's thighs or other weight-related issues. After being around her mother's preoccupation about weight, Lily found herself obsessing again about dieting and exercise. Lily ultimately decided that her continued adult health depended on not seeing her mother very often.

How to Update Your Self-Concept

An accurate self-concept allows you to appreciate your complexity and what you bring to the world as a unique person. To update your self-concept, start with the following:

1. Establish your worth.

2. Identify your values and life philosophy.

3. Fill in the blanks in your self-concept.

4. Define your own self-characteristics.

5. Find role models and mentors.

By working your way through these sections, you'll be surprised at how much you learn about yourself, making your future self-concept much clearer and stronger.

1. Establish Your Worth

The quality of your relationship with yourself and others depends on how much you esteem yourself and your value.

Exercise: How Do You Feel About Yourself?

To find out how you feel about yourself, first sit quietly and try to enter into your deepest feelings. Answer these questions in your journal with the first thing that pops into your mind. Try to respond from your heart, not your intellect.

Am I good?

Am I capable?

Am I enough?

Am I important?

Am I lovable?

Now consider your responses. If you had EI parents, you might have answered one or more of these questions with a no. If so, that's because doubts about self-worth are common results of receiving EI parents' shame and guilt in childhood. The good news is that you can plan to update your self-concept and beliefs about what makes people worthy.

---

2. Identify Your Values and Life Philosophy

The quality of your life will be determined by your underlying values and your understanding of how life works. What would you say are the factors that create a happy, meaningful life? You probably know this subconsciously, but it helps to articulate it. Let's explore some of your beliefs and values.

Exercise: Clarify What You Believe In

There are no right answers in this exercise; just respond with whatever you think. The purpose here is to reveal your underlying personal philosophy and thereby help you know yourself better. Complete the following statements in your journal.

The purpose of life is…

The secret to good relationships is…

Success comes to those who…

You can't have a meaningful life unless you …

The best source of self-esteem is…

I value…

A happy life includes…

It's important to believe…

To get ahead in life, you have to…

It's very wrong to…

The guiding principle I live by is…

People improve themselves by…

These statements get at the heart of how you see yourself and the world, as well as the quality of your relationship with yourself. Once you've completed these sentences, ask yourself how your philosophies may have affected your life course, for better or worse.

3. Fill in the Blanks in Your Self-Concept

Sadly, when a parent doesn't recognize their child's positive qualities, the child doesn't build a self-concept in those areas (Barrett 2017). It's as if a big blank exists where a part of the self should be. For instance, my client Francine could accept praise about her work, but as soon as the compliments were about *her* and her positive personal qualities, she recoiled. She didn't see herself that way, so she immediately made self-deprecating remarks or laughed and made a joke of it.

Francine explained that praise pointed to an inner void she felt in herself: "I don't think of myself as valuable or important. I don't think I matter to people, and I don't think I'll ever be convinced." She recognized that her boyfriend treated her as if she mattered to him, but she couldn't quite believe it. She feared that any minute he would discover she wasn't so great, and then he would see her as "too much trouble." This feeling came from Francine's cold father, who made it clear he didn't have time for her as a little girl. When I asked Francine if she could see herself as a lovable person, she reflected for a moment and then said: "Nope, it's like I've got a hole there. A complete vacuum."

Another client, Caitlyn, was shocked when a member of her church group told her that she "gave the best hugs and was such a good listener." This baffled Caitlyn because, as she told me, "I'm not really a giving kind of person." Caitlyn had learned this distorted self-concept from her depressed and angry mother who was too bitter about life to appreciate Caitlyn's qualities. Caitlyn *was* a giving person, but her mother never saw it.

Although lacking in parental recognition of their best qualities, both Francine and Caitlyn eventually owned their real, but previously unrecognized, good qualities. Francine accepted that she was lovable just for being herself, and Caitlyn realized she was often warm and giving. Both women felt awed and grateful as they accepted being "lovable" and "giving" as real aspects of themselves. Just because their parents never acknowledged those qualities didn't mean they weren't there.

If you got little parental feedback, you too probably have more good qualities than you realize. But like Francine and Caitlyn, if you don't claim these traits in yourself, you might deny your potential with limiting thoughts like: *That's not me. I'm not like that. I'm not the kind of person who...* After a success, you might even say, "I don't know how I did that." But just because you don't recognize something about yourself doesn't mean it's not there. Perhaps it never sank in because nobody ever named it.

With EI parents, you should question any limiting thoughts about yourself; qualities you think you lack, or things you would never try. Is that limitation really true of you, or did it come from the EIPs in your life?

4. Define Your Own Self-Characteristics

EI parents have a poor vocabulary for specific, positive inner attributes. They rarely use descriptive words for the inner psychological world, so they fail to articulate their children's unique qualities and characteristics. Instead, they use vague, generic terms for their children's behavior, such as "good," "bad," "stupid," "smart," or "nice." Consequently, you don't learn enough words for describing yourself or talking about your feelings. This could be a drawback later in life when the ability to articulate your qualities might help you land a job or attract a mate.

Exercise: Put Yourself into Words

Let's start building your more realistic, enhanced self-concept. To get words for describing yourself, you can go online and find a complete list of descriptors for personality characteristics, such as http://www.ongoing worlds.com/blog/2014/11/a-big-long-list-of-personality-traits. You will probably use only a small fraction of these, but it will give you a vocabulary to choose from.

Instead of writing in your journal this time, you may want to use loose sheets of paper so you can write as much as you want on each page and spread the sheets out on a table so you can stand back and see them all at once.

1. *Your family's view of you.* Think about yourself as a child from your family's point of view, including parents, caretakers, and siblings. Write down how you think each person saw you as a child growing up. What adjectives would they use to describe you?

2. *What you now know about yourself.* On a separate piece of paper, write down as many of your current characteristics as you can. Include all your inner qualities and outer attributes.

3. *What you want to become more of.* On another sheet of paper, describe how you want to be in the future. Which characteristics do you want to strengthen, and which tendencies do you want to reduce? What sort of person do you aspire to be as you get older?

Compare these three sheets of paper and write your impressions in your journal. Can you see your trajectory of growth of who you are from past to present to future? Putting yourself into words like this is a great way of appreciating all that you've become and are becoming.

As you go about your day, try on some new words from the online list that capture your characteristics. Look up synonyms of those words and see whether they fit you too. Over time, you will build a better vocabulary to describe yourself. You can also ask friends to contribute: tell them what you're doing, and ask them for words they would use to describe you. Discovering new self-concept words can be an exciting self-validation process for the rest of your life.

---

5. Find Role Models and Mentors

Role models and mentors can help expand your self-concept. If you want to develop yourself, find people you admire and learn from observing them. Spend time with people who have qualities you want to cultivate in your own self-concept. Think of every relationship as an opportunity to become a better version of yourself, and choose companions accordingly.

You might be surprised by how many people are willing to be role models or mentors and pass along their wisdom. If you are enthusiastic about becoming more than you are, look for a mentor who would love to be a part of your journey. For example, take a class with a teacher you like or contact interesting people in local news stories who have inspired you. Figure out what you would like to learn from them so that your requests can be specific.

Call or write those you admire and ask whether they would be willing to answer three *specific* questions about how you could develop more in their areas of strength. If that goes well, you can see whether they would be willing to give guidance and encouragement again sometime when you need it. If you are respectful, specific, and time-limited in your approach, many people will be receptive.

Identify and Challenge Distorted Self-Concepts

It's crucial to uproot and replace distorted self-concepts that you may have gotten from EI parenting. Pay attention to any roles or feelings about yourself that hold you back and challenge them. Here's how to deal with some of the toughest ones.

You Are More Than a Role: Stay Out of the EIP's Dramas

Instead of relating to others as individuals, EIPs lump people into distorted, exaggerated roles. They tend to see every situation as a story populated by victims, aggressors, or rescuers. As they reduce reality to these story lines, EIPs jump to conclusions about who's bad, who's innocent, and who should step in to save them. This distorted role-playing is called the *drama triangle* (Karpman 1968), which is illustrated in the diagram below.

For instance, as a child, Julie frequently got caught up in her mother's drama triangles. She felt guilty for not being able to rescue her mother from her stepfather, whom her mother portrayed as the villain to her role as victim. Julie felt it was up to her to save her mother because no one told her that her adult mother wasn't helpless and could have helped herself.

Aggressor/Villain

Victim/Innocent

Rescuer/Hero

The drama triangle

In another example, teenaged Carla tried to tell her mother that she felt overcontrolled and needed more freedom. Instead of talking with Carla about it, her mother blew up and called her cruel and disrespectful. Her mother portrayed Carla as an aggressor, while she saw herself as the victim. She then expected her husband to rescue her from Carla's "attack" by punishing her.

Seen through a drama triangle, the EIP's distorted narrative of relationships is one of endless conflict: the strong exploit the innocent, who then suffer and deserve to be rescued by someone else. These roles are so easy to fall into, you may not notice it happening. Anyone can get temporarily drawn into these compelling story lines, but EIPs live in them.

The drama triangle feels familiar to us because it is the basis of both children's fairy tales and adult dramas. Good guys and bad guys make riveting plotlines, but in real life, these simplistic, highly emotional themes generate unnecessary conflict and defensiveness. As people polarize into opposing roles, real communication and emotional intimacy stop (Patterson et al. 2012). Look for these story lines whenever EIPs aren't getting their way; their outraged view of events will be straight out of the drama triangle.

If you're not alert to it, drama triangle roles can undermine your relationship with yourself. Think what it would do to your self-esteem if you always saw yourself as a victim. Think how limited your future would look if you always had to be everyone's rescuer. Imagine how you might doubt yourself if you were repeatedly cast as the villain.

The way out of a drama triangle is to see people as responsible for their own behavior and well-being. When you feel pulled into the triangle, you can shake yourself awake and refuse to think of yourself in those roles. You don't have to let your self-concept be defined so one-dimensionally. You aren't limited to being the bad guy, powerless victim, or heroic rescuer. Instead, you can be yourself, think about the overall outcome *you* want, and look for ways to lead the situation in that direction if possible.

Once you stop being fooled by drama triangles, you will be able to relate to people more effectively with less fear or anger. For instance, if an EIP tries to dominate or guilt you, you don't have to accept being their victim. You can take action on your own behalf instead. You can determine what's best for you instead of being blown around by other people's emotional dramas.

Refuse to Be Dominated or Subjugated

If you're okay with others telling you what to think, feel, or do, you are accustomed to being *subjugated* (Young, Klosko, and Weishaar 2003). But subjugation undermines your emotional autonomy and mental freedom and should not be tolerated. Your life isn't theirs to direct, plus it's illogical to think that an EIP knows what's best.

Once you claim your right to make your own decisions and choices, others' attempts at domination will stand out to you as starkly inappropriate. When you have a clear and self-respecting self-concept, your integrity and dignity will no longer allow emotional takeovers and coercions.

There's no need to take someone's attempted dominance seriously; you can simply assert your autonomy by saying things like, "You and I have different opinions on that one," "That's not the choice I want to make," "While that would work for you, that's not my style," or "Thanks, but I can't do that." If the EIP still pressures you, you can say, "I don't have a reason. I'm just not going to."

Any interaction with an EIP that makes you feel disempowered or subjugated is a golden opportunity to strengthen your adult self-concept. If you are tempted to give in to a pushy EIP, remember that you have the right to protect your boundaries. Whenever you feel pressured to give in, take a breath and enjoy the fact that you are free to say no to anything you don't like. You don't have to explain; your preference is good enough. "I don't care to," "No thanks," or "Not for me" can be the absolute end of the conversation.

Question Any Interaction in Which You Feel Inferior or Lacking

Feelings of inferiority can show you exactly where you are mistaken in your self-concept. It's fine to admire other people, but there's something wrong if you see someone as superior to you in *worth*. Try not to idealize or idolize anybody. You can enjoy them more if you stay their equal.

Feeling inferior or unworthy is like a flashing red light letting you know an EIRS or a drama triangle may be sucking you in. If you learn to interpret inferiority sensations as warnings that someone is trying to use you for their own self-esteem needs, you can step back and maintain your autonomy and positive self-concept.

Being around an admired person who is emotionally *mature* will feel different. Instead of making you feel inferior, they will inspire you to pursue your goals. Emotionally mature people show an inclusive, respectful, and coequal attitude toward other people. They elevate you with them, rather than make you feel less than.

Free Your Self-Concept from the Toxic Distortions of Shame

Shame has a special role in distorting your self-concept because, as we saw in chapter 2, shame doesn't seem like an emotion, it feels like who you *are*. This has serious consequences for your self-concept.

Shame is such an excruciating experience that it makes people want to disappear, sink through the floor, or die of embarrassment. Remember from chapter 2 that when parents treat you as if you're bad, your self-concept can be burdened with what psychologist Jerry Duvinsky (2017) calls a *core shame identity*.

But feelings of shame don't tell a truth about you, and it's important to clear this up. The only truth about shame is that an EIP probably made you feel awful about yourself at an age when you were psychologically defenseless. As an adult, you can defuse shame feelings by exposing the erroneous self-belief that underlies it, looking at it without running away, and then questioning it. Duvinsky (2017) points out that repeatedly exploring childhood shame feelings and then relabeling them correctly—as highly unpleasant emotions, not the truth of you—shrinks shame back into a manageable emotion, not a declaration of your worth as a human being.

By questioning shame, you can unmask it as just an *emotion* foisted on you by others, instead of being your core *identity*. Instead of absorbing shame into your self-concept, you could treat it as just another emotion. Here's how to do that.

Exercise: Take the Sting Out of Shame

Think of something you have felt ashamed about. As you revisit the moment, keep reminding yourself this is just an *emotion* you're feeling, not something bad about you. Duvinsky (2017) recommends writing down how the shame feels, while repeatedly relabeling it as nothing more than a painful emotion. Tell yourself, "This feels awful, but it's just a feeling. It could never, ever be a statement of who I am. This feeling of shame is just an emotion, like any other emotion." By facing it this way, shame becomes just another painful feeling you can easily survive.

Once you face these feelings, twinges of shame will no longer feel so catastrophic. You may even see shame as a helpful warning that someone is trying to make you feel bad so they can feel better about themselves. Seeing shame for what it is not only helps free you from others' emotional coercions but repairs your self-concept as well.

Affirm Your Self-Concept as a Loving Person

EIPs see you as cold and uncaring if you don't jump into their problems with both feet. If you hesitate to sacrifice yourself for them, they call your basic goodness into question. They can make you think you're not loving enough.

Doubting your capacity for love is one of the most damaging self-distortions that can come out of your relationship with EI parents. Your inability to save them, make them happy, or make them feel loved enough can make you worry you might be emotionally lacking. For example, one woman grew up believing her heart was like a "frozen pea," while another said she feared dating because men would see there was "not enough" to her. Both these people had emotionally insatiable EI parents who never validated how emotionally generous their hearts really were.

Just because an EI parent can't appreciate your efforts at love doesn't mean you aren't loving. They often just can't accept it, or it's never enough. Don't tie your worth or goodness to whether an EI parent feels loved by you. Instead, channel more love and appreciation into your relationship with yourself. With an EI parent, you will surely need this extra self-support.

Realize the Emotional Costs of a Diminished Self-Concept

Many people have lived with a negative self-concept so long that they can no longer feel how it affects them. Instead of feeling indignation or hurt feelings, these people have conditioned themselves to accept subjugation and disrespect. This dulls the pain of being treated badly, but it's important to awaken to the high cost of a low self-concept. Once they finally realize how painful it is to feel so diminished by others, they can do something about it. As Tony Robbins (1992) has described, sometimes the best way to motivate yourself to change is by deliberately *amplifying* how painful the old way is.

For instance, let's say you laughed along with family members who made fun of you in an unkind way, just as they did in your childhood. You could just brush it off as a familiar script you've played a million times, but what if you stopped and intentionally *felt* how the derogatory remarks emotionally affected you? What if you realized what it was like to be scared to defend yourself or, worse, to laugh along with your tormentors? If you really let it sink in, you might begin to feel compassion for yourself. Keep amplifying the feelings until you realize how destructive those experiences are to your self-esteem and your trust of others. By feeling your hurt and the compassion it arouses, you begin to see yourself differently.

Change is easier when you really *feel* the magnitude of what your old distorted self-concept has cost you. That's when your pain can be used for good.

How Does It Feel to Have a Healthy Self-Concept?

A positive self-concept gets a good start from a parent's connection and loving support. But there is also an individual spark in each of us that supports resilience and self-recovery no matter what your history (Vaillant 1993). Perhaps it comes from an intimate relationship with yourself, in which you just *know* you are destined for more. Some of us, even in the absence of nurturing relationships, seem to have mysterious inner resources that allow us to be our own conscious companion, enabling us to learn and grow our way out of adverse circumstances. This source of inner friendship with ourselves can give us self-care, self-comforting, and even self-protective instincts against exploitative people.

You'll know you have a healthy self-concept when you have gotten to know yourself and found yourself good. You will cherish your individuality—your interests, your passions, your ideals—plus those new strengths you're working on. With a healthy self-concept, you are not obsessed with correcting what's *wrong* with you. You're just trying to fulfill your potential and become more genuinely yourself. You have a healthy self-concept when your individuality is precious to you, and you don't want to be anybody or anything other than who you are. This kind of self-concept is your birthright as a human being.

Highlights to Remember

Your self-concept is your knowledge of who you are and what you're like. Unfortunately, growing up with EI parents, you may have developed a distorted self-concept that encourages feelings of inferiority and subjugation. EI relationships can trap you in distorted self-concepts, such as feelings of being an imposter or one-dimensional drama triangle roles. But you always have the option to reclaim your autonomy and authority, in spite of feeling less than others or encountering blank spots in your self-concept. By trusting your inner self-guidance and finding mentors and role models to channel your development, you can build an enhanced and healthier self-concept.

Chapter 10

Now You Can Have
the Relationship
You've Always Wanted

Just Focus on One
Interaction at a Time

You can create healthier relationships with your EI parents by thinking about what you are willing to accept, one interaction at a time. Time spent with your EI parent will be more productive if you keep your mind on the immediate interaction instead of the whole relationship at once. It's too much pressure to try to have a good *relationship* with them; just try for one constructive *interaction* in the moment. The key is to relate to your EI parent more honestly and actively, instead of keeping quiet and allowing them to take over or getting into an argument with them. As long as you maintain a secure self-connection and awareness of EI tactics, you won't be so vulnerable to EI coercions.

By being loyal to yourself and your inner world, you maintain your boundaries, emotional autonomy, and right to your own individuality. As you put your self-connection first, you'll be capable of a new kind of relationship with your parents—one in which you're much more self-aware and self-protective. In many ways, this will be the relationship you've always wanted because it's the relationship in which *you can finally be yourself around them.*

It hasn't just been about how they treated you, it's also about how you've overlooked yourself in order to get along with them. It's as if you unwittingly "signed" a relationship contract with them in childhood without realizing what it would cost you in your adult life. Thankfully, you can now revise that old relationship arrangement to be fairer to you. Your new awareness of their level of emotional maturity will enable you to see what they're doing, and ask yourself whether you want to change how you respond.

Even if you are out of contact with your parents or they are no longer living, you can still use your memories to imagine relating to them differently. By mentally redoing previous interactions, you can even change how the past feels to you. One woman told me that reimagining calmer, more autonomous responses to her father had given her the best relationship she had had with him in years—and he had been dead for seven of those.

Now let's review the unspoken agreement you may still have with your EIP or EI parents and come up with better terms.

Do You Want to Keep Your Old EI-Relationship Contract?

Most relationships build up unspoken agreements over time, but we usually don't become aware of them until there's a problem. These "contracts" mostly remain hidden, but by bringing them out in the open, you can see what you've been agreeing to. The following exercise can help you become aware of what you may have been going along with and see whether you still want to follow those terms.

Exercise: Reevaluate the Terms of Your EIP Relationship

Apply the following statements to a significant EIP in your life and in your journal write "agree" or "disagree" for each one.

1. I agree that your needs should come before anyone else's.

2. I agree not to speak my own mind when I'm around you.

3. Please say anything you want, and I won't object.

4. Yes, I must be ignorant if I think differently from you.

5. Of course you should be upset if anyone says no to you about anything.

6. Please educate me about what I should like or dislike.

7. Yes, it makes sense for you to decide how much time I should want to spend with you.

8. You're right, I should show you "respect" by disowning my own thoughts in your presence.

9. Of course you shouldn't have to exercise self-control if you don't feel like it.

10. It's fine if you don't think before you speak.

11. It's true: you should never have to wait or deal with any unpleasantness.

12. I agree: you shouldn't have to adjust when circumstances change around you.

13. It's okay if you ignore me, snap at me, or don't act glad to see me: I'll still want to spend time with you.

14. Of course you are entitled to be rude.

15. I agree that you shouldn't have to take direction from anyone.

16. Please talk as long as you like about your favorite topics; I'm ready to just listen and never be asked any questions about myself.

The point of this exercise is to make you aware of how you may have unwittingly allowed your EIP to take over as the most important person in the relationship. By exposing these relationship terms, it'll help you be more aware of what you are willing to go along with in the future.

Two Thoughts That Will Rebalance Any Interaction with an EIP

Unfair EI relationship patterns can be rebalanced with two new thoughts that will vastly improve your interactions with any EIP. When there is conflict or you feel emotionally coerced by an EIP, do the following:

1. See yourself as equal in importance to them. ("I am just as important as they are.")

2. Keep a conscious self-connection and accept yourself unconditionally. ("I have good stuff inside me.")

Recalling these two facts—you are just as important as they are, and you have good stuff inside you—blocks any EIP's attempt at coercion or entitlement. When you remember these two things, your interaction with an EIP will feel different. The EIP may continue to do what they do, but if you see yourself as equally important and stay self-connected, you'll have a completely different relationship experience. When you exercise these foundational attitudes, you can't be dominated, separated from yourself, or fooled into thinking that your experience is not as important as theirs.

1. You Are Equal in Importance to Them

EIPs can't imagine that anybody's needs are as important as theirs. Because they feel entitled to a position above you in the relationship hierarchy, they assume you too will accept their primacy. Such confidence can give them an air of authority and even charisma, but their self-assurance originates in egocentricity and emotional immaturity. Fortunately, now you can see through such self-centered assumptions.

Your self-reconnection begins as soon as you start wondering what exactly makes them a more important person than you. As you ponder this question, you will discover that there *isn't* a reason why they're more important than you; it's just the feeling you get.

Once you see yourself as equal in importance—in spite of their behavior to the contrary—you'll naturally think of more active and assertive responses. You'll ask for what you prefer in the moment. You'll respond in ways that gently remind them: "I'm here too, and my needs matter as much as yours." You'll explain what would be best for *you* without shame or apology because there's nothing shameful about being on an equal footing.

2. You Keep Your Self-Connection and Accept Yourself Unconditionally

By honoring the worth of your inner self and inner world, you'll feel a new security and contentment. When you accept yourself as you are and stay connected with your immediate experience in this moment, you'll feel stronger inside. When you love yourself as an evolving being, it feels right to protect your energy and interests. No longer will you dissociate from your own feelings in order to make EIPs the center of your attention. It'll feel unacceptable to put your needs on hold just because they like to come first.

It's important to resist the urge to shrink yourself into a tiny space inside yourself when you're around the EIP. It's wrong for you to take up as little room as possible just so they can expand. This shriveling of your value is a leftover childhood defense and should come to an end. By protecting your right to your own thoughts and feelings, you stay present. Instead of shrinking and becoming their obliging audience, you can remain "full of yourself."

How to Keep Your Self-Connection and Stay Present

The only way an EIP can take over your emotional and mental life is to get you to disconnect from your inner life. When EIPs spellbind you into passivity, they induce emotional immobility and dissociation from yourself. Now, however, you can use mindfulness to reverse that process.

Being mindfully conscious of yourself may look like you're not doing anything—you may even be silent—but it is a huge accomplishment because it keeps you from going along with the EIP's expectation that you exist to serve their self-esteem and keep them emotionally stable. Mindfulness is so psychologically effective because it gives you a tool for resetting your mindset from passive to intentional.

If you dedicate yourself to mindful self-awareness *while in the EIP's presence,* you will regain your emotional autonomy, mental freedom, and the right to be yourself. It's hard to overestimate the liberation you give yourself when you intentionally focus on your own feelings and thoughts when in close physical proximity to an EIP.

You can practice this by looking an EIP in the eye while deliberately remaining aware of all your own thoughts and feelings. See what it feels like to be fully present inside even as they expect you to be focusing on them. This intentional self-awareness is an audacious rejection of the old relationship contract because they are no longer the center of your attention. This emotional autonomy and freedom of thought is well worth practicing so you stop automatically giving up your self-possession in their presence.

Instead of fixating on what the EIP wants, pay attention to your body sensations, your immediate emotional experience, and your thoughts. By paying attention to what you are directly experiencing in this moment, you are no longer putting the EIP first.

You might want to try Thich Nhat Hanh's (2011) mindfulness practices, which are extremely practical and easy to use. For instance, you can stay self-connected by focusing on your breath and saying to yourself, "Breathing in, I am here. Breathing out, I am calm." Attending to your breathing helps you remember that you are present and have value, even as the EIP tries to make the interaction all about them.

By practicing these new attitudes and approaches, you shift your interactions with your EI parent toward being about two people instead of one. Next we'll look at more ways to accomplish this.

How to Steer Your EIP Relationships Toward More Equal and Peaceful Interactions

No relationship is satisfying unless you can be genuine. In this next section, we are going to look at ways to interact with an EI parent that will raise the chances of real connection with them, yet not leave you feeling that you let yourself down.

Interrupt Old Patterns Before They Take Over

To avoid emotional takeovers, pay attention when an EIP puts pressure on you to take responsibility for validating or fixing their feelings. When you experience that tug to make them feel better at your own expense, you can interrupt the takeover by staying aware of what they're doing. It also helps to narrate their behavior with self-talk like the following:

Now they're trying to emotionally coerce me and make me feel bad.

Now they're inviting me to spin up into their drama triangle.

Now they're on the "me" channel. Every topic goes back to them.

Now they're dismissing and disrespecting my inner experience.

Now they're questioning my right to have my own feelings and thoughts.

Now they're challenging my duty to take care of myself first.

Now they're making me feel guilty so they can seem blameless.

Once it becomes second nature to spot these dynamics, you can respond in new ways to protect your boundaries and emotional autonomy. EI takeovers are most easily dissipated as soon as they begin. At first, EIPs can "make" you feel things, but as you become more conscious of what they're doing, their attempts lose power.

For instance, my client Tina felt a sensation like "a twig snapping" inside her when she finally reached a breaking point over her mother's victimized complaining. From then on, Tina changed the subject, objected, or left whenever her mother started burdening her and draining her energy. Once Tina became aware of the toxic effect of some of her mother's conversation, she could dodge it as automatically as if she were avoiding physical blows. ("Mom, I don't have the skills to help you with that. Let's talk about something else.") If her mother had persisted in asking her to just "listen," Tina could've said something like, "Can't do it, Mom. It makes me too sad."

Interrupting emotional takeovers means that you say what you feel, ask for what you want, and set boundaries on what you don't like. By immediately speaking up about what you need in the moment—*however tentatively or awkwardly*—you step out of roles that keep your EIP interactions shallow and full of stress.

Become the Relationship Leader

Once you interrupt the EIP's control, you can try to move the interaction toward the outcome you want. By suggesting preferable outcomes, you lead the way toward a more equal and respectful adult relationship. For instance, when a parent tries to take over or give advice, you might say: "Well, that's a good idea, Mom, but it's important to let me think this through for myself." If a parent gets angry and speaks harshly, you can be the leader by saying: "I expect you to control yourself. We're two grown adults now. How are we going to have a respectful adult relationship with you talking to me like that?"

Relationship leaders model respectful behavior and teach reciprocity in their interactions. They are explicit about how they want to be treated and what feels relationally rewarding for them. Relationship leaders spell out supportive values that inspire people to treat each other well.

For example, Brie was a great cheerleader to her father, who was trying to lose weight, celebrating his every success. But when Brie had a fitness goal of her own, her father never asked how it was coming along. Brie told her father that support should be a two-way street, that it would be more fun for both of them that way. Her father seemed surprised—as if he had never thought of that—and promised to show more interest.

It's self-defeating to follow EIPs when they are not mature enough to be responsible leaders. It's not doing them any favors if you *know* a better way but don't *teach* them a better way.

Improve the Relationship One Interaction at a Time

Interactions are better managed when you aren't worrying about the overall quality of your relationship. Handling an interaction is doable, but improving a relationship is too big a goal. By focusing on only one interaction at a time, you will feel much more effective and less discouraged.

In fact, try going into an interaction with your EI parents in a neutral frame of mind, as if you had no history with them at all. Let it be a brand-new day. Pretend everything they say and do is something you've never experienced before, such that you are free to respond genuinely in the moment. This technique of entering interactions freshly—"without memory or desire" (Bion 1967)—lets you meet people where they are without seeing interactions through old resentments. You don't hold old stuff against them and you see them with new eyes. You can interact with your parents as if they were acquaintances you had recently met socially—*having no expectation that they would meet your deeper emotional needs.* You don't have to love them, and they don't have to love you. You can just get along.

One woman told me how much better her connection was with her mother since she had laid aside any expectations for a close relationship. Instead, she interacted pleasantly with her mother as just another interaction with an elderly person. This woman realized that she actually had stopped needing anything from her mother years ago. In fact, her current emotional life felt perfectly satisfying whether her mother loved her or not. Now she accepted each little interaction with her mother on its own terms without comparing her mother's behavior to what she used to wish for. Once she decided to treat each interaction as a new moment, without grudges or hope, feelings of bitterness faded. She felt satisfied with whatever interactions they had.

Mature Communication Keeps Your Interactions Real

Keeping interactions real means you use *clear, intimate communication* to tell the other person in a nonattacking way what you are feeling and thinking, and what you truly want. Clear, intimate communication is not rude or confrontational. It neutrally states your experience and does not blame, interpret, or threaten. You're not trying to change them: You're just telling them how their behavior affects you. You are communicating clearly how the relationship is going for you, and thereby making it safe for them to open up as well if they want to. By being transparent about your inner experience, you participate honestly in the relationship and let yourself be known. Things immediately get more real between you.

To Have a More Genuine Relationship, Express Yourself

Telling EIPs and EI parents how something made you feel is a giant step toward being loyal to yourself. By staying in touch with yourself and relating to them as a coequal, you change the terms of your relationship. Your interactions become more emotionally intimate and genuine, even if only from your side. Every time you speak up—in whatever uncomfortable or hesitant way you can manage to do it—you bring about more meaningful communication and pull the relationship out of stagnating in superficiality.

Your self-expression demonstrates your equal status. When you speak up, you're showing equal status to the other person. By expressing yourself, you are saying that what goes on inside you is just as important as what goes on inside the EIP. Thus, you don't let EI hierarchies form.

Expressing yourself around EIPs can be a challenge, however, because they usually don't ask questions or leave many openings for you to participate. You might have to make a space to speak by interjecting things like, "Wait!" or "Hang on!" or even raising and waving your hand. If they interrupt, you can say, "Just one more minute, I'd like to finish," then take a comfortable breath before you go on. Whether they listen to you is *not* the point. The important thing is that you are taking action on your own behalf by requesting to be heard. Your relationship with yourself will be strengthened regardless of how they respond.

Ask them to listen to you. If you get upset with an EIP about something and can't manage to say anything at the time, you can always go back to them later and ask if they'd be willing to hear you out. Tell them you have some thoughts to share and ask if they'll give you five minutes. (The five-minute limit is important because emotional intimacy makes them so nervous.)

If they agree, relate your experience by describing their *specific* behavior, how it made you feel, and ask what they were intending. ("Dad, when you scowled and your face got red, I felt like you were shutting me down. It felt like I'd better not share what I think. I felt like I didn't have a right to an opinion. Do you want me to keep quiet around you? What do you want me to do when you look angry like that?")

In each five-minute conversation, talk about only one interaction. Keep a respectful, curious, and nonaccusatory attitude as you spell out the feelings you got from their behavior. If they interrupt or want to argue, you can acknowledge them, but ask them to let you finish.

When the five minutes is up, thank them for listening to you and ask them if they want to tell you anything. They may not want to, but remember, your mission was accomplished as soon as you asked to talk. That act alone reversed your old childhood role. By sharing your concern, you changed your old relationship contract (such as "I agree not to speak my mind around you"). Short talks like this show both of you that your connection can survive some honesty and leave things feeling more real.

I can't stress enough that even if such a communication effort doesn't fix the issue you raised, it has already done its job: you acted like an equal and took the lead with clear, intimate communication. This is a huge step forward.

Use Skillful Nonjudgmental Communication Instead of Confrontation

Fortunately, we know a lot now about what kinds of communication promote positive outcomes under stressful circumstances. Productive communication styles are honest, nonjudgmental, neutral in tone, and empathetic to the other person's viewpoint. Let's look at the kinds of communication styles that are likely to work best with EIPs and EI parents.

Noncomplementary communication. This style of communication, described by Professor Christopher Hopwood (2016), responds to angry or aggressive behavior in an unexpectedly calm and empathetic way. The surprise of its kindliness often derails hostility or attempts at dominance. When the upset person encounters curiosity and sympathy instead of a counterattack, the inevitability of conflict is turned upside down.

To use this approach, you respond to the EIP's hostility with empathy as if they were looking for understanding rather than a fight. By discerning their deeper emotional desire for connection, you interpret their unpleasant behavior as a cry for attention and acceptance. Sometimes the surprise of an empathetic response transforms a belligerent situation and instead allows something creative, meaningful, and connecting to take place.

For instance, Bobbi's partner always came home from business trips in a grouchy mood. Bobbi finally figured out her partner was not only tired, but afraid that Bobbi wouldn't be glad to see her. The next time Bobbi's partner came through the door looking like a thundercloud, Bobbi got up, gave her a hug, and said, "I'm so glad you're back. I've missed you. Would you like something to eat?"

Other people skilled in noncomplementary communication use humor or disarming friendliness to defuse tense situations so that anger doesn't get any traction. An innocent and concerned response can also make an EIP's aggressive intent fizzle. For example, when they give you unfair criticism, you might reply with a neutral, "Oh, I didn't know that." Noncomplementary communication lets you respond to their need to be understood instead of just reacting to their hostile actions. If done sincerely, a noncomplementary response can transform an unpleasant confrontation into a moment of surprising connection. Even angry people just want to be seen and acknowledged.

Nondefensive and nonviolent communications. Nondefensive (Ellison 2016) and nonviolent (Rosenberg 2015) communications are methods of dealing with people in ways that don't attack, humiliate, accuse, or shame. The goal of these methods is to listen without becoming defensive while still knowing what matters to you.

Nondefensive, nonviolent communication keeps you out of the polarizing aggressor-victim positions of the drama triangle. You recognize that the other person's viewpoint makes perfect sense to them. At the same time, you talk about your intentions in a way that doesn't challenge their worth. By responding nondefensively, you don't trigger an aggressor-victim drama triangle. You make the other person feel like it's safe to keep communicating.

These skillful styles of communication recognize both people as having legitimate intentions and highly meaningful needs. Using these communication skills can take the emotion and judgment out of discussions with EIPs. Regardless of the EIP's response, you will feel far more effective and in control of yourself when you use them. In addition to the authors cited above, other helpful books can be found in the references section of this book to learn more about open, nonthreatening styles of communication (Patterson et al. 2012; Stone, Patton, and Heen 1999).

When Differences Cause Conflict

Now let's look at how to handle unavoidable disagreements. How can we handle boundary violations or unacceptable actions and still have the best possible relationship?

Set boundaries and say no. In any relationship, refusals and boundaries are necessary to protect your well-being. You don't have to make excuses or give explanations. You can just say, "No, I really can't," or "That won't work."

Unlike normally sensitive people, however, EIPs make it hard to refuse them. They may question your refusal by saying things like, "*Why* can't you do it?" Or they might try to problem solve your decision, saying, "Well, couldn't you do it if you…?" followed by a suggestion. No reasonably polite person would keep on like that, but EIPs act like your time belongs to them. If they still persist after you refuse, you can say: "Do you need me to give you more reasons? I'm afraid I can't," or just give them a helpless shrug.

Accept only as much as you want. EIPs are often generous in ways that make you feel trapped and obligated. They focus on what they want to give, regardless of whether you want it. For instance, EIPs and EI parents may give gifts *they* would like to get, insist on get-togethers you don't enjoy, plan unwanted activities, or repeatedly offer help you don't want. Just as children keep begging with, "Again!" EIPs don't sense that other people may be getting tired or not enjoying an activity as much as they are. One man, after his mother wouldn't take no for an answer about bringing a gift over, finally explained to her, "Mom, your gifts don't feel like gifts. They feel like obligations."

If you don't make a fuss over what they are offering—whether it's food, gifts, money, hospitality, or advice—they act like you're being rude and deliberately hurting their feelings. But of course, this is untrue. You have the right to say, "That's all," or "That's enough" about anything. Same for, "No more," or "Wish I could, but no thanks." After that, it's up to them to handle their feelings.

Don't reward regressive behavior. EIPs and EI parents will often sulk or act wounded, prompting you to rescue them. If you jump in to pacify them, you are encouraging more regressive, guilt-inducing behaviors.

For instance, my client Sandy had a very emotional mother, Cora, who would withdraw in tears to her bedroom when something happened she didn't like. Sandy usually felt bad and followed after her mother, asking her questions and trying to make her feel better. Sometimes Cora would prolong this attention by refusing to talk or accept comforting until Sandy had persisted for several minutes.

Sandy was understandably tired of this pattern, so she tried something new. The next time Cora did this, Sandy went to her bedroom and said *sincerely*, "I can see you're really sad, Mom. I'm going to let you work it out. When you're ready, I'll be downstairs, and we can go shopping like we planned. But I want you to take as much time as you need to feel sad." Sandy then gently closed the door after her.

With this new approach, Sandy gave autonomy to her mother and stepped out of the rescuer role. Sandy empathized with Cora's feelings— she wasn't cold or critical—but let her know this wasn't something she could participate in or fix for her. Cora came downstairs about fifteen minutes later, and Sandy smiled at her and said, "Ready to go shopping?"

In another example, Paul's rigidly moralistic father refused to go out to dinner as planned because he thought Paul had finagled a reservation under false pretenses. Paul told his father calmly, "That's fine, Dad. Please don't do anything you don't want to. We're going to leave in about a half hour. If you change your mind, we'd love to have you go with us, or you can catch a cab over later if you'd like to join us for coffee and dessert."

The important thing in these examples is that there was no blame, shame, or attempt to change the parent's emotion. These parents were given autonomy to have their feelings and make their choices. They could go along with a fun outing, or they could stay upset. They were respectfully offered options.

Express anger clearly, directly, and with respect. While calm interactions are ideal, there are times when anger feels necessary. An EI parent's stubbornness can be very hard to take, especially when there's been a long history of dominance by this parent. Fortunately, your anger can still be expressed in a respectful, nonabusive way.

———Bethany's Story———

Bethany began her session one day by announcing, "I blew up at my dad today." It turns out her elderly EI father, Levi, had berated the staff at his nursing home yet again, yelling at them for small oversights as if he were in a five-star hotel. Now several of the aides were threatening to walk off his case. Bethany had had enough of the phone calls about her father's behavior. She needed him to understand the seriousness of the situation. She confronted Levi with the facts by reminding him that if he kept this up, he might get kicked out and end up in a much less nice place (which was true; he had limited funds and had been lucky to find the place he was in).

Bethany reminded him the staff had tough jobs and were people too. She told him she was tired of always having to patch things up for him and that he should think of others for a change. "I'm exhausted," Bethany told him. "You have to think of what all this is doing to me. What are you going to do if I'm dead? Show some gratitude, Dad! Take some of the burden off me. You know how to be nice, so do it!"

Bethany didn't shame or abuse Levi; she simply communicated forcefully what she needed him to do. Levi was of sound mind, so he wasn't excused from decent social behavior, even at this late date. He didn't like his circumstances, but Bethany didn't like hers either. For Bethany's own health, she needed to tell Levi to make an effort and stop creating more work for her. This confrontation didn't change Levi's personality, but it opened a moment of clarity and clear intimate communication between them. To Bethany's amazement, her father later apologized. They became—for the moment—two adults working something out between them.

Bethany showed how anger can be expressed forcefully, but as clear, intimate communication instead of an attack. Every time her dad slipped back into abusive behavior, Bethany now had an active way of expressing her displeasure and telling her dad what was expected of him. Maturely handled anger may be emotional and intense, but it stays on topic and deals *directly* with the other person about a *specific* issue. Ross Campbell (1981) describes how anger can be expressed at many different levels of maturity and in ways that are more or less conducive to resolving a problem. The anger may be negative in tone, but as long as it is expressed logically, in words, on topic, without abusive language or behavior, and is directed only at the person or problem in question, it's still at a pretty mature level.

Bethany's tone with her father was emotional and negative, but she was still addressing the problem objectively and telling him what she needed without becoming abusive. She wasn't trying to punish or dominate him; she was just raising the volume to be heard through his self-preoccupied fog. She forcefully reminded him that there are other people in the world, and if he didn't take them into consideration, he might lose the support he was taking for granted. It was good for both of them that Bethany put her foot down and kept it real between them.

Accepting Your Losses and Going Forward

Many people think that a good relationship with their parent means the parent would finally be happy with them. But considering the dissatisfaction and defensiveness of EIPs, you know that nothing keeps them happy for long. Why not give up trying to change them and instead become happy with yourself? By accepting the EIP's limitations, you become freer to take care of yourself and may even feel more compassion for them.

Appreciate What You Can and Honor Whatever Bond You May Feel

Most of us feel a primal attachment to our parents, regardless of whether our emotional needs were met. Family connections run deep regardless of frustrations, and not many of us want to relinquish these bonds completely. Even exasperating family relationships can feel meaningful and irreplaceable at a basic human level. Strong feelings of belonging create powerful ties to our parents in spite of painful or depriving experiences with them.

One woman told me that she still wanted a relationship with her mother, even though her mom wasn't "gentle, soft, or safe." This woman remembered vividly the moment, crying in her bedroom, when she realized her mother was never going to change. At that moment, she resolved to accept her mother as she was because the family connection was so important to her.

Another woman had had a very difficult and vexing relationship with her EI father. She had been treated badly and let down many times by him. But when he became terminally ill, she was by his side constantly. After he died, she realized that her conflictual feelings about him no longer seemed to matter. "He was my *dad*," she said.

Your EI parents may not have given you all the love you needed, but they played an essential role in *your* learning to love, and that is also an important thing. So of course you may feel very attached to your parents—just don't forget to stay equally attached to yourself as well. As long as you don't give yourself up to keep a relationship with them, it will be all right.

Seeing Your Relationship with Your EI Parent Now with Compassion and Realism

Once you free yourself from EI relationship patterns that held you back, you may regret the time you lost before you became more self-aware and sure of your capacity for love. Many people wish they could have back the time they spent trying to accommodate their parents' distortions and craving their approval. But perhaps it can comfort you to know that once you are free of oppressive EI relationship control, you really do get a new life to live. The difference is sometimes so marked between past enthrallment to EI parents and a newly developed self-possession that it's as if you got to have two lives and two self-concepts instead of one.

As you look back on your relationship with your EI parents, you may regard your parents with both compassionate sadness and steely realism. You now have a broader perspective in which you can finally stand outside the relationship and view it as an adult.

———Grace's Story———

Grace had worked hard in therapy to develop a more positive self-concept and a more socially rewarding life. She had grown up with a dominant mother who was so mistrustful and controlling that Grace felt disloyal if she did much outside the family. After her mother's death, Grace became more socially open and found that people were much kinder and more welcoming than her mother had been. Grace didn't grieve for her mother—there was too little closeness for that—but thinking back on her mother's life, she did feel compassion for how much her mother's emotional immaturity had cost her.

"I don't think any of us kids grieved my mom because she was so cold. She lost out by not being beloved. Most of her children had terrible struggles with her. She had such a lack of empathy; she seemed to have an absence of wanting to be connected to you. She was so committed to her thought processes of judging people and how they fell short that she couldn't love anybody. She focused on how people should be improving themselves. She just didn't have the ability to connect with the heart song of another person. She could be compassionate at a theoretical level, like at church, but on a personal level she was so difficult. Everything was about what was done to *her*, not empathy for us. Her resentment caused such ugliness in her that she couldn't be loved because of how she acted."

I found Grace's growth over time and her awareness of her mother's emotional limitations profoundly moving. Grace's growth trajectory followed the path of many people who have recovered from EI parents. As Grace became attached and loyal to herself, she discovered what she was interested in and whom she liked. She loved her home and pets, and enjoyed more friends and meaningful group activities. Now that Grace felt free to choose the life directions that spoke to her, she could see clearly how her mother's fears had fenced in her life. She felt compassion for her mother, but she was relieved her life belonged only to her now. Grace's nurturing relationship with herself was becoming all that she had never gotten from her mother.

Grace had developed a new understanding of her mother, all these years after her mother's death. She could see her mother objectively because she now had a loving and protective relationship with her inner self, the innocent part of her who had loved her mother even when her mother couldn't love her back. Grace felt more whole now, like her own person, not because she finally won her mother's love but because she had found herself.

Once you free yourself from EI relationship patterns that held you back, you may regret trying so hard with people who gave so little in return and hurt you so much. As you become more aware of your worth and capacity for love, it may pain you to realize how poorly you were treated.

Many people wish they could regain the time they spent trying to adjust to their parents' egocentrism and craving their approval. But perhaps it can comfort you to know that finally understanding and accepting EIPs as they are frees you from trying to please or change them, allowing you to fully enjoy your own emotional autonomy, inner experiences, and freedom of thought. You can't get your childhood back, but the rest of your life is now yours to create. With a new foundation in your inner self, it will surely be a beautiful thing.

Highlights to Remember

Now that you have thought deeply about the impact of EI people in your life, you can reconsider relationship terms you no longer want. You realize now you're equal in importance to any EIP, and you can stay connected to yourself and your inner world in loyal, loving, and self-protective ways. In your relationship with your EI parents, you now can be genuine about your own needs, limits, and rights to self-expression—even anger at times. You now know how to actively respond to EIPs in ways that leave you feeling whole and empowered. You can honor your deep family bonds with them, yet still protect your autonomy and freedom to be who you really are. Once you can fully be yourself and feel equally important, no emotionally immature relationship system can take you over. In its place are two people meeting each other as equals—the EIP and you—now with a much better chance of having a real relationship between two very different individuals.

Bill of Rights for Adult Children of Emotionally Immature Parents

As we come to the end of our journey, I want to leave you with a bill of rights to refer back to whenever you face challenges in an EI relationship. These ten basic rights summarize what you've learned in this book, especially the idea that you are entitled to your own life. Please use them as a shorthand summary of how to stay centered when dealing with EI parents and other EIPs. I hope you will find them helpful. I wish you the very best in reclaiming your emotional autonomy, mental freedom, and inner life. My hope for you is that as a result of reading this book, you will use the insights gained here to derive maximum growth and self-discovery from any future EIP interactions you may have.

1. The Right to Set Limits

I have the right to set limits on your hurtful or exploitative behavior.

I have the right to break off any interaction in which I feel pressured or coerced.

I have the right to stop anything long before I feel exhausted.

I have the right to call a halt to any interaction I don't find enjoyable.

I have the right to say no without a good reason.

2. The Right Not to be Emotionally Coerced

I have the right to not be your rescuer.

I have the right to ask you to get help from someone else.

I have the right to not fix your problems.

I have the right to let you manage your own self-esteem without my input.

I have the right to let you handle your own distress.

I have the right to refuse to feel guilty.

3. The Right to Emotional Autonomy and Mental Freedom

I have the right to any and all of my feelings.

I have the right to think anything I want.

I have the right to not be ridiculed or mocked about my values, ideas, or interests.

I have the right to be bothered by how I'm treated.

I have the right to not like your behavior or attitude.

4. The Right to Choose Relationships

I have the right to know whether I love you or not.

I have the right to refuse what you want to give me.

I have the right not to be disloyal to myself just to make things easier on you.

I have the right to end our relationship, even if we're related.

I have the right not to be depended upon.

I have the right to stay away from anyone who is unpleasant or draining.

5. The Right to Clear Communications

I have the right to say anything as long as I do so in a nonviolent, nonharmful way.

I have the right to ask to be listened to.

I have the right to tell you my feelings are hurt.

I have the right to speak up and tell you what I really prefer.

I have the right to be told what you want from me without assuming I should know.

6. The Right to Choose What's Best for Me

I have the right not to do things if it's not a good time for me.

I have the right to leave whenever I want.

I have the right to say no to activities or get-togethers I don't find enjoyable.

I have the right to make my own decisions, without self-doubt.

7. The Right to Live Life My Own Way

I have the right to take action even if you don't think it's a good idea.

I have the right to spend my energy and time on what I find important.

I have the right to trust my inner experiences and take my aspirations seriously.

I have the right to take all the time I need and not be rushed.

8. The Right to Equal Importance and Respect

I have the right to be considered just as important as you.

I have the right to live my life without ridicule from anyone.

I have the right to be treated respectfully as an independent adult.

I have the right to refuse to feel shame.

9. The Right to Put My Own Health and Well-Being First

I have the right to thrive, not just survive.

I have the right to take time for myself to do what I enjoy.

I have the right to decide how much energy and attention I give to other people.

I have the right to take time to think things over.

I have the right to take care of myself regardless of what others think.

I have the right to take the time and space necessary to nourish my inner world.

10. The Right to Love and Protect Myself

I have the right to self-compassion when I make mistakes.

I have the right to change my self-concept when it no longer fits.

I have the right to love myself and treat myself nicely.

I have the right to be free of self-criticism and to enjoy my individuality.

I have the right to be me.

Acknowledgments

My sincere thanks go to Tesilya Hanauer, my acquisitions editor, who originally saw the promise in the concept of emotionally immature parents. Tesilya was committed to shepherding this book through its lengthy development process, and her patience, tenacity, and belief in the book have made it possible for everything I discovered with my clients to reach the public. Much appreciation also goes to New Harbinger editors Clancy Drake and Jennifer Holder, who worked so tirelessly on refining the book's focus and organization so that everything was expressed as clearly as possible. Many thanks too for the keen eye and guidance of copyeditor Gretel Hakanson.

I stand in awe of my many clients who agreed to let me use their disguised and anonymous material with "if it can help someone else, sure!" We discovered together how to move from the confusion of growing up with EI parents to the lightness of being that comes from deeply understanding what you've been up against and transforming constricting patterns into new strengths.

My gratitude also goes to the theorists and researchers of developmental psychology, who made possible my understanding of emotional immaturity and its effects. I was fortunate that my graduate work exposed me to the developmental and personality insights of the old masters of psychology, instead of focusing only on symptoms and techniques. Theories show us the big picture and make sense of it all. I learned from the best.

I want to thank my colleagues Brian Wald, Tom Baker, and Mary Warren Pinnell, whose ideas and suggestions were immeasurably helpful to me during the writing of this book as I picked my way through thorny issues and puzzling points.

I am deeply grateful for the emotional support and enlightening discussions that came from my sister, Mary Babcock, who has been my biggest supporter since childhood. Her insights and deep understanding of people's behavior always help me get to the bottom of things. Thanks too to Barbara and Danny Forbes, for their ideas and contributions. Barbara sees my heart and has given me constant love and special celebrations over many years.

Lynn Zoll has been both nurturer and cheerleader throughout this process, keeping me laughing by sending poems, food, and "Write on!" emails, while always being available to talk over book points. Kim Forbes has also been unfailing in her interest, support, and uniquely inspiring cards and texts, not to mention our enlightening discussions. My deep thanks too to Esther Freeman, who in our long friendship has taught me so much about responding actively to setbacks and discouragements. Her invaluable insights always steer my ideas toward practicality and application.

Thank you to my wonderful son, Carter Gibson, who has kept tabs on my progress and lifted me up with fresh and encouraging takes on what seemed like overwhelming setbacks. I love the way he sees the world and does his life. I wish his kind of aliveness for everyone.

Finally, deepest thanks of all go to my husband, Skip. My connection with him has been the joy of my life and has been a primary catalyst for whatever emotional maturity I may have. He supported my dream for this book both emotionally and materially, but the best part was his deep understanding of the importance and power of dreams themselves.

References

Ainsworth, M., S. Bell, and D. Strayton. 1974. "Infant-Mother Attachment and Social Development: 'Socialization' as a Product of Reciprocal Responsiveness to Signals." In *The Integration of a Child into a Social World*, edited by M. Richards. New York: Cambridge University Press.

Barrett, L. 2017. *How Emotions Are Made: The Secret Life of the Brain*. New York: Houghton Mifflin Harcourt Publishing Company.

Beattie, M. 1987. *Codependent No More*. San Francisco: Harper and Row.

Berne, E. 1964. *Games People Play*. New York: Ballentine Books.

Bickel, L. 2000. *Mawson's Will*. South Royalton, VT: Steerforth Press.

Bion, W. 1967. "Notes on Memory and Desire." *Psychoanalytic Forum* 2: 272–273.

Bowen, M. 1985. *Family Therapy in Clinical Practice*. Lanham, MD: Rowman and Littlefield Publishers, Inc.

Bowlby, J. 1979. *The Making and Breaking of Affectional Bonds*. New York: Routledge.

Bradshaw, J. 1990. *Homecoming*. New York: Bantam Books.

Burns, D. 1980. *Feeling Good*. New York: HarperCollins Publishers.

Campbell, R. 1977. *How to Really Love Your Child*. Wheaton, IL: SF Publications.

Campbell, R. 1981. *How to Really Love Your Teenager*. Colorado Springs: David C. Cook/Kingsway Communications.

Capacchione, L. 1991. *Recovery of Your Inner Child*. New York: Touchstone.

Clance, P. R., and S. Imes. 1978. "The Imposter Phenomenon in High Achieving Women: Dynamics and Therapeutic Intervention." *Psychotherapy Theory, Research and Practice* 15 (3): 241–247.

Clore, G. L., and J. R. Huntsinger. 2007. "How Emotions Inform Judgment and Regulate Thought." *Trends in Cognitive Sciences* 11 (9): 393–399.

Degeneres, E. 2017. "Holiday Headphones." December 5. Ellentube.com. https://www.youtube.com/watch?v=78ObBXNgbUo.

DeYoung, P. A. 2015. *Understanding and Treating Chronic Shame*. New York: Routledge.

Duvinsky, J. 2017. *Perfect Pain/Perfect Shame*. North Charleston, SC: CreateSpace.

Ellison, S. 2016. *Taking the War Out of Our Words*. Sunriver, OR: Voices of Integrity Publishing.

Ezriel, H. 1952. "Notes on Psychoanalytic Group Therapy: II. Interpretation." *Research Psychiatry* 15: 119.

Fonagy, P., G. Gergely, E. Jurist, and M. Target. *Affective Regulation, Mentaliztion, and the Development of the Self*. New York: Other Press.

Forbes, K. 2018. Personal communication.

Forward, S. 1989. *Toxic Parents*. New York: Bantam Books.

Fosha, D. 2000. *The Transforming Power of Affect*. New York: Basic Books.

Fraad, H. 2008. "Toiling in the Field of Emotion." *Journal of Psychohistory* 35 (3): 270–286.

Frankl, V. 1959. *Man's Search for Meaning*. Boston, MA: Beacon Press.

Gibson, L. C. 2015. *Adult Children of Emotionally Immature Parents*. Oakland, CA: New Harbinger Publications.

Goleman, D. 1995. *Emotional Intelligence*. New York: Bantam.

Gonzales, L. 2003. *Deep Survival*. New York: W. W. Norton and Company.

Gordon, D. 2007. *Mindful Dreaming*. Franklin, NJ: The Career Press.

Goulding, R. A., and R. C. Schwartz. 2002. *The Mosaic Mind*. Oak Park, IL: Trailhead Publications.

Hanson, R. 2013. *Hardwiring Happiness*. New York: Harmony Books.

Hatfield, E. R., R. L. Rapson, and Y. L. Le. 2009. "Emotional Contagion and Empathy." In *The Social Neuroscience of Empathy*, edited by J. Decety and W. Ickes. Boston: MIT Press.

References

Hopwood, C. 2016 "Don't Do What I Do." NPR. *Shots: Opinion: Your Health*, July 16. https://www.npr.org/sections/health-shots/2016/07/16 /485721853.

Huntford, R. 1985. *Shackleton*. New York: Carroll and Graf Publishers.

Jung, C. G. 1959. *Aion: Researches into the Phenomenology of the Self*. Princeton, NJ: Princeton University Press.

Kabat-Zinn, J. 1990. *Full Catastrophe Living*. New York: Bantam Books.

Karpman, S. 1968. "Fairy Tales and Script Drama Analysis." *Transactional Analysis Bulletin* 26 (7): 39–43.

Katie, B. 2002. *Loving What Is*. New York: Three Rivers Press.

Kernberg, O. 1985. *Borderline Conditions and Pathological Narcissism*. Lanham, MD: Rowman and Littlefield Publishers.

Kohut, H. 1971. *The Analysis of the Self*. Chicago: University of Chicago Press.

Kornfield, J. 2008. *Meditation for Beginners*. Boulder, CO: Sounds True.

Mahler, M., and F. Pine. 1975. *The Psychological Birth of the Human Infant: Symbiosis and Individuation*. New York: Basic Books.

McCullough, L. 1997. *Changing Character*. New York: Basic Books.

McCullough, L., N. Kuhn, S. Andrews, A. Kaplan, J. Wolf, and C. Hurley. 2003. *Treating Affect Phobia*. New York: The Guilford Press.

Minuchin, S. 1974. *Families and Family Therapy*. Cambridge, MA: Harvard University Press.

Nhat Hanh, T. 2011. *Peace Is Every Breath*. New York: HarperCollins Books.

Ogden, T. 1982. *Projective Identification and Psychoanalytic Technique*. Northvale, NJ: Jason Aronson, Inc.

O'Malley, M. 2016. *What's in the Way Is the Way*. Boulder, CO: Sounds True.

Patterson, K., J. Grenny, R. McMillan, and A. Switzler. 2012. *Crucial Conversations*. New York: McGraw-Hill.

Perkins, J. 1995. *The Suffering Self*. New York: Routledge.

Porges, S. 2011. *The Polyvagal Theory*. New York: W. W. Norton and Company.

Robbins, T. 1992. *Awaken the Giant Within.* New York: Free Press.

Rosenberg, M. 2015. *Nonviolent Communication.* Encinitas, CA: Puddle-Dancer Press.

Schore, A. 2012. *The Science of the Art of Psychotherapy.* New York: W. W. Norton and Company.

Schwartz, R. 1995. *Internal Family Systems Therapy.* New York: The Guildford Press.

Siebert, A. 1993. *Survivor Personality.* New York: Vantage Books.

Simpson, J. 1988. *Touching the Void.* New York: HarperCollins.

Smith, M. 1975. *When I Say No I Feel Guilty.* New York: Bantam Books/Random House.

Stern, D. 2004. *The Present Moment.* New York: W.W. Norton and Company.

Stone, D., B. Patton, and S. Heen. 1999. *Difficult Conversations.* New York: Penguin Group.

Stone, H., and S. Stone. 1989. Stone. *Embracing Ourselves.* Novato, CA: Nataraj Publishing.

United Nations. 1948. "Universal Statement of Human Rights." http://www.un.org/en/universal-declaration-human-rights.

Vaillant, G. 1977. *Adaptation to Life.* Boston: Little Brown.

Vaillant, G. 1993. *The Wisdom of the Ego.* Cambridge, MA: Harvard University Press.

Van der Kolk, B. 2014. *The Body Keeps the Score.* New York: Viking/Penguin Group.

Wald, B. 2018. Personal communication.

Wallin, D. 2007. *Attachment in Psychotherapy.* New York: The Guildford Press.

Whitfield, C. L. 1987. *Healing the Child Within.* Deerfield Beach, FL: Health Communications, Inc.

Wolynn, M. 2016. *It Didn't Start with You.* New York: Penguin Books.

Young, J., J. Klosko, and M. Weishaar. 2003. *Schema Therapy.* New York: The Guilford Press.

Lindsay C. Gibson, PsyD, is a clinical psychologist in private practice who specializes in individual psychotherapy with adult children of emotionally immature (EI) parents. She is author of *Who You Were Meant to Be*, and writes a monthly column on well-being for *Tidewater Women* magazine. In the past, she has served as adjunct assistant professor of graduate psychology at the College of William and Mary, as well as at Old Dominion University. Gibson lives and practices in Virginia Beach, VA.